W9-CBU-207

HEALING DRUGS

FACTS ON FILE SCIENCE
SOURCEBOOKS

HEALING
DRUGS

THE HISTORY OF PHARMACOLOGY

MARGERY AND HOWARD FACKLAM

Facts On File, Inc.

Facts On File, Inc.
11 Penn Plaza
New York NY 10001

Library of Congress Cataloging-in-Publication Data
Facklam, Margery.
    Healing drugs : the history of pharmacology / Margery and Howard Facklam.
        p. cm.—(Facts on file science source books)
    Includes bibliographical references and index.
    Summary: Traces the history of pharmacology, from the early days of leeches and simple plants to modern research into drugs to work against cancer.
    ISBN 0-8160-2627-0
    1. Pharmacology—History—Juvenile literature. [1. Pharmacology—History.] I. Facklam, Howard. II. Title. II. Series.
    RM301.17.F33   1992
    615'.1'09—dc 20   9198

Facts On File books are available at special discounts when purchased in bulk quantities for businesses, associations, institutions, or sales promotions. Please call our Special Sales Department in New York at 212/967-8800 or 800/322-8755.

Text design by Ron Monteleone
Jacket design by Amy Gonzalez
Composition by Facts On File, Inc./Ron Monteleone
Manufactured by The Maple-Vail Book Manufacturing Group
Printed in the United States of America

On the cover: Two doctors who work for a pharmaceutical company examine a film showing the nucleic acid sequence of a natural immunosuppressant. Trying to harness the body's own defenses for use in medicine is one of the aims of today's researchers.

You can find Facts On File on the World Wide Web at http://www.factsonfile.com

10 9 8 7 6 5 4 3

This book is printed on acid-free paper

This book is for Matthew Scott Facklam,
with love from his grandma and grandpa.

ACKNOWLEDGMENTS

Collecting—and understanding—information for this book would not have been possible without help. We are grateful for the time and patience of the following experts in the field of drug design and development, especially when we asked them to repeat explanations again and again: Dr. Wayne K. Anderson, professor in the department of medicinal chemistry at the State University of New York at Buffalo; Dr. Thomas J. Facklam, director of research and development at Aries-Serono Pharmaceutical Company, Geneva, Switzerland; and David P. Facklam, clinical research manager at Chugai-Upjohn, Rosemont, Illinois. We appreciate Paul H. Facklam's skillful illustrations and the bulletins from Jeannene Tylee at Johns Hopkins Center for Alternatives to Animal Testing.

Margery and Howard Facklam
Clarence Center, New York

CONTENTS

1 SIMPLES AND LEECHES

Have a headache? Take an aspirin—or any one of dozens of other painkillers on the drugstore shelves. Americans take 16,000 tons of aspirin tablets each year—that's 80 million pills. They spend about $2 billion a year buying nonprescription painkillers that contain aspirin or aspirinlike drugs.

If you'd lived thousands of years ago and complained of a headache, a witch, priest, or tribal healer might have cured you with a tea brewed from the bark of a willow tree. If the willow-bark tea didn't relieve your headache, the healer might have put a pair of leeches on either side of your forehead to draw out blood and relieve the pressure. Or you might have been given a tea made from the ground-up gallbladder of a bear or the ground-up brains of an owl.

A dose of earthworms rolled in honey was used as a cure for an upset stomach in some cultures. The brain of a sheep was said to be good for insomnia, fox lung for treating tuberculosis, deer heart for heart disease, and cow dung and moldy bread poultices for stopping infections.

But plants made up the most common household remedies. Herbal medicine is as old as humankind, and for some remote tribes, it is still the only source of treatment. Every culture had its medicine men and women, witches, or priests who kept the secrets of the potent narcotics, poisons, hallucinogens, and other magical remedies. As long as ignorance kept people enslaved to superstition, the idea of magical plants remained powerful.

What people were ignorant about, of course, was the cause of disease. Knowing nothing of germs, or how the body functioned, people tended to believe that illness was punishment from the gods for breaking the laws and taboos of the community. A disease was thought to be caused by the curse of an enemy getting revenge or by a specific god who had control over a part of the body. The causes of battle wounds, insect bites, or broken bones were easy to see and understand, but generally people were convinced that disease came from evil forces entering the body.

In Chinese mythology there's a story about three demons who bring malaria. One demon carries a hammer to cause a pounding headache. The second carries a pail of icy water to chill the victim, and the third carries a stove to produce a fever.

No wonder people believed powerful medicine was necessary to drive out an evil illness. Even now there are those who think that if the medicine tastes awful, it must be strong and therefore will do a good job. In almost every culture, healers mixed their medicines with onions, garlic, urine, excrement, or other foul-smelling or strong-tasting stuff. In the 17th century, a favorite medicine was "Elixir Universale." It contained gold, powdered lion's heart, witch hazel, earthworms, dried human brains, and Egyptian onions. Until the early 1900s in America, it wasn't unusual to send kids to school with a string of garlic around their neck to ward off colds. If it worked, it was probably because no one got close enough to sneeze in the face of the garlic-wearer.

But how did people know which plants or animal parts would heal? Who tested them? How did they know that one plant would soothe an upset stomach or another draw out the poison of an infection? Who volunteered to drink a brew of bark, berries, or gallbladder? Imagine how difficult it must have been to find the right dose, the one that healed instead of killed.

People do recover—some of them, anyway—from even the worst diseases. There are very few illnesses that leave no survivors. Most diseases tend to kill some and spare others. So a healer in any age had some successes.

Drugs from Plants

Two hundred years ago, Horace Walpole read a poem about three princes from the land of Serendip (now Sri Lanka) who made discoveries they weren't looking for, and he invented the word *serendipity* to mean a lucky discovery. A lot of trial and error and a lot of serendipity has gone into finding medicines. Sometimes by a lucky accident a healer hit upon the right part of the right plant, the right dose at the right time—like willow bark to relieve pain. And when he or she did, that recipe became part of that healer's *materia medica,* or list of ingredients for medicine.

Every Native American tribe had its healing herbs and rituals. The Zuni Indians of the American Southwest believed the gods gave them 14 different plants that could cure a stomachache by causing the patient to vomit.

The Polynesians, who canoed across the Pacific Ocean 2,000 years ago and settled in the islands of Hawaii, took trusted medicinal plants with them. One was the awapuhi-kuahiwi, or wild ginger. They ground up the thick underground stems of the wild ginger, mixed it with water, and strained it to make a clear liquid that soothed a stomachache. We use the same ingredient when we sip ginger ale to settle an upset stomach.

For centuries, the Indians of Peru and Ecuador have used the sap from curare vines to poison the tips of their arrows and darts to paralyze or kill animals or human enemies. They even have a system of grading the curare. If a monkey struck by a poisoned arrow has time to get from one tree to another before it falls, that curare is top-grade. It is "one-tree curare." "Two-tree curare" works slowly enough to let the monkey get to two trees, and "three-tree curare" is definitely of poor quality.

Curare blocks the nerves that move muscles, first in the arms and legs and then in the rib cage, which leaves the victim unable to breathe. When researchers realized that curare causes complete relaxation of the muscles, rather than a rigid paralysis, they knew they had found a useful drug. The purified active ingredient from curare is given to patients to induce muscle relaxation before surgery, which makes it easier for surgeons to operate.

Not all of the old recipes worked, of course. In ancient Rome, a scholar known as Pliny the Elder wrote about a treatment for boils. He told a patient to take nine grains of barley, trace a circle around the boil three times with each grain, then throw the barley into the fire with the left hand for an immediate cure.

Even the most educated Romans believed in witchcraft medicine, and those beliefs carried right through to the Middle Ages (from around the 5th century into the 15th century). But by then, the Christian church had put down the pagan ideas, and discovery meant certain death for a witch, even a "good" witch, who knew the healing recipes. So the old Roman formulas remained secret. Plants were gathered at a certain phase of the moon, and often they were mixed with the blood of bats, vipers, or toads, which added to the magic of the medicine.

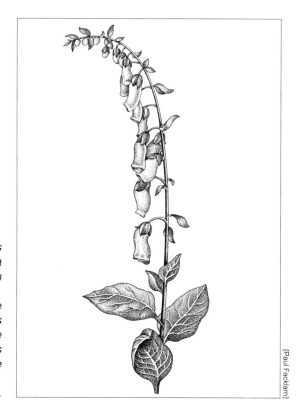

The tall beautiful stalks of foxglove contain a deadly poison that can stop a heart or keep it going. Foxglove's active ingredient, digitalis, is used to strengthen the heart and regulate its beat. No human-made drug has been found that works as well.

[Paul Facklam]

Henbane was a standard ingredient in any witch's brew. All parts of this roadside weed are poisonous. Even the smallest bite of it will cause dizziness, confusion, blurred vision, and convulsions. Too big a dose causes a slow, painful death. For the healer brave enough to find a safe dose, henbane was a good sedative, and a poultice of the mashed leaves of henbane eased the pain of rheumatism.

But the ancient healers had no idea why a plant could heal or harm. It is only in the last 50 or 60 years that chemists have begun to discover all the acids, sugars, alkaloids, starches, gums, resins, tanin, oils, mucilage, vitamins, steroids, minerals, traces of metals, and other active ingredients in plants.

Today the U.S. Food and Drug Administration (FDA) classifies henbane an unsafe plant. But since scientists discovered henbane's effective ingredients, the plant has become one source of a narcotic and muscle relaxant called scopolamine or "truth serum," and of a drug called atropine, which is used to dilate the pupil of an eye during examination.

The ancient healers guessed right when they used willow bark to soothe aches and reduce fevers. In 1899, German chemists analyzed the bark of *Salix alba*, the willow tree, and found its active ingredient, salicylic acid. They called it aspirin, but even then they didn't know how or why it worked as a painkiller. That chemical secret was not discovered until the 1980s.

Just as we have first-aid supplies in our medicine cabinets, every housewife from the Middle Ages on kept a garden of healing herbs known as "simples." Along with cooking herbs, they planted medicinal herbs such as comfrey, belladonna, foxglove, garlic, and periwinkle.

Comfrey's botanical name, *Symphytum,* means "grown together." Used in ancient Rome and Greece, this herb has been called knitbone, bruisewort, and knitback. A poultice or pack of comfrey's crushed leaves promotes the healing of broken bones and soothes bruises. Its active ingredient is allantoin, now used in ointments to treat skin rashes.

For centuries, foxglove was used to treat everything from epilepsy to tuberculosis, but it is also a deadly poison. A leaf of foxglove chewed and swallowed can cause paralysis and sudden heart failure.

(Paul Facklam)

Henbane has been called devil's eye and also poison tobacco because all parts of the plant are poisonous. But this common weed is also a source of atropine, scopolamine, and other sedatives.

5

HEALING DRUGS

In 1775, an English doctor, William Withering, found that foxglove would strengthen a failing heart. And since then, foxglove has been the source of digitalis, which is still the drug most often used to regulate and strengthen the heartbeat.

Garlic is more than a seasoning for food. It's been a medicinal herb for thousands of years, used to fend off both diseases and devils. In August, 1990, 50 scientists from 15 countries met for the First World Congress on the Health Significance of Garlic and Garlic Constituents in Washington, D.C. Their topic was garlic as a cancer preventive.

A single berry from the deadly nightshade contains enough poison to kill a person. This common weed's scientific name is *Atropa belladonna*. *Belladonna* means "beautiful woman" in Italian. In the past, women used a drop of juice from this plant to dilate the pupils in their eyes to make them look more beautiful. Today the juice from belladonna is used to make atropine and other drugs.

Jimsonweed is a close cousin of the nightshade, and just as deadly. One sip of its juice or a few of its seeds can kill. Farmers try to keep their pastures free of jimsonweed so horses and cattle won't eat it. But now drug manufacturers use the active ingredient of jimsonweed as another source of atropine and scopolamine. It is so important as a

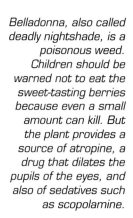

Belladonna, also called deadly nightshade, is a poisonous weed. Children should be warned not to eat the sweet-tasting berries because even a small amount can kill. But the plant provides a source of atropine, a drug that dilates the pupils of the eyes, and also of sedatives such as scopolamine.

(Paul Facklam)

basic ingredient for drugs that during World War II, when it was difficult to import jimsonweed, the Eli Lilly Company raised its own supply on farms in Indiana.

In convent and monastery gardens in the Middle Ages, nuns and monks tended the medicinal herbs and gave help to anyone who came to be healed. But the "golden age" of herbals really came about when explorers went out from Europe and returned with new medicinal plants used by the people in other lands.

Missionaries living in South America in the 1600s were surprised to find that the Peruvian Indians knew how to treat malaria, a disease that has probably killed more people than all wars combined. Malaria is spread by *Anopheles* mosquitoes. The mosquitoes inject the malaria parasite into the bloodstream, causing headache, high fever, chills, nausea, anemia, and fatigue.

Ancient cures for malaria consisted of prayers, purging, potions made of the eyes of crabs, and herb pills coated with gold. In one monastery, a prescription for treating malaria written in the 1200s said,

> *Take the urine of the patient and mix it with some flour to make a good dough thereof, of which seventy-seven small cakes are made; proceed before sunrise to an anthill and throw the cakes therein. As soon as the insects devour the cakes the fever vanishes.*

If this recipe cured, it was mostly by luck.

[Eli Lilly Company]

During World War I, pharmaceutical companies raised their own crops of belladonna. This field of belladonna in Greenfield, Indiana, belonged to the Eli Lilly Company.

7

The Peruvian Indians, however, treated malaria successfully with a medicine they made from the "fever bark" trees that grew on the eastern slopes of the Andes Mountains. An Augustinian monk living in Peru in 1633 wrote,

> In the district of the city of Loxa grows a certain kind of large tree, which has bark like cinnamon, a little more coarse, and very bitter; which, ground to powder, is given to those who have fever, and with only this remedy, it [the fever] leaves them.

He was describing chinchona trees.

The Jesuit priests, who lived among the Incas for many years, sent ground chinchona bark to Europe, where it was known as "Jesuit's powder." Many Protestants refused to touch it, even though an English physician, Dr. Thomas Sydenham, wrote,"Of all the simples, Peruvian bark is the best." But when Dr. Robert Talbor cured King Charles II of malaria in 1668 by using chinchona, his fame spread and so did the use of the amazing medicine.

Two French chemists extracted the active ingredient in chinchona bark in 1820. Their first attempt had failed because they had used the bark of the wrong chinchona tree. There are more than 50 different kinds of chinchona trees, and only a few produce the healing substance. When the chemists tried bark from the yellow chinchona, they got a pale yellow gummy substance that was definitely a new chemical. They chose the name *quinine,* from *quinquina,* which was the Peruvian Indian name for the bark. The new drug was pure, potent, and dependable, but it was very expensive to produce. Quinine was the first chemical compound used successfully against an infectious disease.

For 5,000 years, the Chinese have used extracts from the leaves of the ginkgo tree to treat coughs, asthma, allergies, and heart and lung diseases. Like other ancient remedies, the medications worked but no one knew why until the 1980s, when chemists at Harvard University isolated a compound they call ginkgolide B, which is very effective in treating asthma and circulatory problems.

Another of the simples, a pretty garden flower called the Madagascar periwinkle, or vinca rose, was used by healers around the world. In Hawaii, the plant was boiled and the extract was used to stop bleeding. In India, wasp stings were soothed by juice from periwinkle leaves. In South and Central America, the juice was used as a gargle for sore throats. In America in the 1950s, researchers found two anticancer drugs in periwinkle—vincristine and vinblastine. Both inhibit the growth of tumors, but vincristine works best against childhood leukemia, and vinblastine is used to treat Hodgkins' disease.

Drugs from the Animal Kingdom

About half the prescription drugs in the United States are still made from simple plants, but animals are also used. Insulin, the drug that treats diabetes, was made originally from the pancreas glands of cattle, pigs, goats, and sheep, and vaccines are made from antibodies built up in the blood of horses and rabbits.

The slimy leech was once a standard treatment for a variety of ailments, from mental illness to gout, tumors, and whooping cough. When a medicinal leech feeds, it presses its three jaws of razor-sharp teeth against the victim's skin and cuts through it like a circular saw. The wound looks like a three-rayed star. The leech's salivary glands produce hirudin, a substance that numbs the wound and prevents the blood from clotting. A single leech can suck up about a tablespoonful of blood before it feels full and drops off, but an equal amount of blood will continue to flow before it clots.

Leeches are still used to relieve black and blue spots, especially around the eyes. But they've also become a source of a drug that helps heart attack victims. Hirudin is collected from giant Amazon leeches that are raised on leech farms. Then a substance called hemetin is extracted from the hirudin. Hemetin dissolves blood clots after they form, and it can stop the progress of a heart attack and limit its damage.

The saliva of the vampire bat also contains a protein that prevents blood from clotting. When a vampire bat lands on a warm-blooded animal, it makes a small bite in the animal's skin, and then laps up the blood with its tongue. As long as the bat keeps licking the open wound, the blood flows because of a protein in the bat's saliva. Scientists call this substance Bat-PA, for plasmogin activator, which like hemetin, has great possibilities for treating heart attacks.

If the ancient healers could step into a drug research laboratory today, they wouldn't recognize the modern equipment, but they might feel right at home among the simples, leeches, bat blood, and goat glands still used to make medicines.

2 THE PLANTS OF JOY AND SORROW

The poppy was just another garden flower until someone found the secret of opium, the most ancient painkiller. There are dozens of different kinds of poppies, but only *Papaver somniferum,* the poppy that grows in warm, sunny climates, yields the milky juice used to make the best commercial opium. It's called the white poppy, but its petals can be white, red, mauve, or purple.

For thousands of years, farmers in India, Africa, China, Asia Minor, and Mexico have gathered the dried juice from unripe seedpods of this white poppy. They used—and still use—the poppy seeds to flavor food, and the fine oil pressed from the seeds has been prized by artists for hundreds of years. But opium is the main product of these plants. On clay tablets made in Babylon in 4000 B.C. the poppy was called "plant of joy." In ancient Greece, the whole poppy plant—leaf, stem, flower, seedpod—was boiled to make a sleeping potion called *meconium.* The juice scraped from the seedpod was called *opus,* meaning sap. From that comes the word *opium.*

Hippocrates, the "father of medicine," the man whose words every doctor repeats when he or she takes the Hippocratic oath, discouraged the use of opium because it was too powerful. But his warning did not stop people from using opium as a poison, a medicine, and especially as a pleasure drug.

In the second century B.C., one remedy for toothache was a mixture of opium, black pepper, saffron, carrot seed, aniseed, and parsley seed. Another early medication made from opium was an anesthetic that was called a "surgical sleeping draught." By the 1660s, an English physician, Thomas Sydenham, wrote of opium that "there is not one that equals in its power to moderate violence of so many maladies and even to cure some of them." He mixed opium with saffron and wine to make a drug he called laudanum, which was widely used right into the early 1900s. Benjamin Franklin praised laudanum, which he took to ease the pain of kidney stones.

Morphine

In 1803, Frederick Wilheim Sertuerner extracted the pure, odorless, but bitter crystals of opium. He chose the name *morphine,* for Morpheus, the Greek god of dreams. After he tested the extract on dogs, Sertuerner used himself as a guinea pig—and almost died in the process. Later he convinced three brave men to take a smaller dose of the "magic crystals" of morphine as a further test that it was safe for humans.

Morphine was the first chemically active ingredient to be extracted from a plant, and it was a huge step forward in making drugs. Once the active ingredient of a crude drug was known, drug manufacturers could design more accurate doses. They could get rid of impurities and control a drug's toxic effects. But most important, as chemists began to learn the exact chemical structure of a drug's active ingredient, they could synthesize it from other chemicals.

Codeine

In 1832, another drug, called codeine, was extracted from opium. Both morphine and codeine work on the central nervous system. Morphine relieves severe pain, but the patient remains conscious and doesn't lose hearing, speech, vision, or sense of touch. All other pain relievers are measured against morphine as the standard. It is carried in every ambulance in case someone is pinned in a wreck, or badly burned, or having heart failure. Morphine dilates blood vessels and prevents fluid from backing up into the lungs when the heart is failing. Both opium and morphine are in the U.S. Strategic and Critical Materials Stockpile, quickly available for war or natural disaster.

Codeine is a bit less powerful than morphine as a painkiller. But in 1983 (the year for which the most recent figure is available) codeine was the key ingredient in 65 million prescriptions, and the number-one prescription sold in American drugstores was Tylenol with codeine.

But long before morphine or codeine were found, European explorers and settlers brought crude opium to North America. Used alone or dissolved in alcohol, opium was the accepted and expected treatment for hundreds of years. One historian says that compared to the bleedings, blisterings, purgings, and other heroic treatments of the time, opium was cherished by both patients and doctors. A booklet called the *American Dispensatory,* written in 1818, pointed out opium's "extraordinary value" in treating a wide range of diseases from cholera to asthma. But this booklet was also one of the first to report that the constant use of opium could lead to "tremors, paralysis, stupidity, and general emaciation."

In order for a drug to do its work, it has to reach the bloodstream. The more directly it gets into the blood, the faster it works. Many people had tried to make some kind of needle for injections, but it wasn't until 1853 that Dr. Alexander Wood perfected a hypodermic syringe. When the Civil War began 10 years later, this quick method of injecting morphine was a blessing to wounded soldiers. But Dr. Wood probably wished he had never invented it because his wife was the first person to become addicted to morphine-by-needle. She died from an overdose.

Heroin

In 1874, Heinrich Dresser, who was a scientist at the German Bayer Works, created still another drug from opium—one he claimed was much safer than morphine and not at all addictive. It was actetyl-morphine, but when the Bayer Company introduced it in 1889, they called it heroin. It turned out to be one of the most addictive and dangerous of all drugs.

Once it gets into the body, heroin quickly breaks down into morphine again. When it's injected into a vein, there's an overpowering rush and sensation of pleasure—but that doesn't last long. Addiction comes quickly. Addicts who don't get another rush of heroin become nauseated and their bodies hurt all over. Although it's not easy, that physical feeling can be overcome in a week. The psychological addiction is worse. Addicts want heroin so desperately that they'll do anything to get it, and that feeling of need can stay with them for life. Heroin is illegal in the United States, yet it is estimated that Americans spend $4 billion a year buying it. The United States also imports tons of legal opium for medicinal morphine and codeine, mostly from India.

Cocaine

Cocaine also comes from an ancient herb. "In certain valleys, among the mountains, there grows a certain herb called Coca, which the

Indians do esteem more than gold and silver. The virtue of this herb found by experience is that any man having these leaves hath never hunger or thirst . . ." That journal entry was written in 1555 by a Spanish explorer, Augostin De Zarate. He had seen native Indians of Peru working 36 hours at a stretch in the gold and silver mines, high in the Andes Mountains, without sleep, food, or water.

The "divine plant of the Incas" is the coca tree, *Erythroxylon coca,* a woody shrub with shiny green leaves and red berries, not to be confused with Brazil's cacao tree that gives us cocoa and chocolate. In an old journal, an entry was found describing the conquered native people who were forced to work in the mines. The traveler wrote that "coca chewing helped them to endure, to forget, and to escape their misery." Actually, the people did not chew the leaves, but packed them between their teeth and cheeks, where the leaves mixed with saliva.

Three hundred years passed after that observation before anyone knew how the coca leaves worked their magic. In 1860, a German scientist, Albert Niemann, extracted the active ingredient from coca, and called it cocaine. It was greeted as a wonder drug. One American doctor claimed that cocaine was no more habit-forming than tea or coffee. He made "cocaine wine" from two grains of cocaine to a pint of wine and claimed that it could cure both alcohol and opium addiction.

In hot disagreement, two German doctors pointed out the horrible side effects of chewing coca leaves. The Peruvian Indians had greenish, broken-down teeth, dazed eyes, an unsteady walk, general apathy, and incurable insomnia. And Europeans who had taken to the new fashion of chewing this drug found they could not stop using it. But few people paid any attention to the doctors' warnings.

In Paris, Dr. Angelo Mariani tried to raise coca trees in his garden. But they didn't grow, so he imported tons of coca leaves from South America to make his amazing new products, which he claimed would cure headaches, depression, indigestion, and insomnia. Soon doctors were praising Mariani wine, Mariani lozenges, powders, and teas, and some even went so far as to say they had used the products to cure anemia, gout, tuberculosis, malaria, goiter, convulsions, and syphilis. Dr. Mariani was honored by Pope Leo XIII, who was only one of the doctor's famous satisfied customers.

But not everyone agreed on the goodness of cocaine. In the late 1800s Dr. Thomas Moreno y Maiz, who had been chief surgeon in the Peruvian army, did some experiments to prove how destructive cocaine could be. He put an equal number of fat, healthy rats in two

(American Institute of the History of Pharmacy Collection, Kremers Reference Files, Madison, WI 53706)

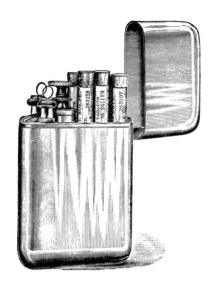

In 1894, there were many drug kits on the market. The Parke-Davis Company emergency kit held hypodermic syringes, cocaine, morphine, atropine and strychnine.

cages. He fed one group of rats coca leaves, and fed the other group nothing. The rats that ate the coca leaves died before the rats that had been left to starve! It was true that chewing coca leaves did overcome fatigue, thirst, and hunger. But Dr. Moreno y Maiz could not convince people that it was cocaine's ability to dull those needs that made the drug seem so amazing. Coca was an anesthetic.

Even the famous psychiatrist Sigmund Freud believed in this wonder drug. He wrote, "I can assure you that cocaine is absolutely harmless, even in long use. It is an absolute antidote for morphine addiction. Why, with cocaine in our hands, we can dispense entirely with asylums for addicts." Three years later, when a close friend of his became horribly addicted, Freud realized that cocaine could do more harm than good.

Not everything about cocaine was bad, however. When Niemann had isolated cocaine from the coca leaves, he had tasted it and noticed it made his tongue numb. Several others—a Viennese doctor, a Russian physiologist, and a Peruvian doctor—also wrote papers about the ability of cocaine to numb, or anesthetize. In 1884, Dr. Carl Koller tested cocaine's numbing ability, first on frogs and guinea pigs, and then on himself. Koller put a few drops of cocaine in his eye and then allowed a friend to touch that eye with a pin. When he felt nothing, Koller knew he had the perfect anesthetic for eye surgery.

A German chemist, Alfred Einhorn, discovered another use for cocaine in 1904. He used it as a spinal anesthetic and called it novocaine. During World War I, when the United States took over many German patents, novocaine was renamed procaine.

The use of cocaine raced through America. How could there be anything bad about a product that made people feel so good? Legitimate drug companies packaged and sold it. The Parke-Davis Company made 15 forms of cocaine, including coca cigarettes, cocaine for sniffing, and cocaine for injection. They advertised their handy cocaine kit, with the drug that "can supply the place of food, make the coward brave, the silent eloquent and . . . render the sufferer insensitive to pain."

Cocaine found its way into all kinds of products. The most famous is the drink made by John S. Pemberton. In 1885 he started a company in Atlanta, Georgia to produce Coca-Cola. He advertised it as "the intellectual beverage . . . valuable brain tonic and a cure for all nervous affections." Its no wonder his drink took the country by storm. It contained cocaine, along with caffeine from kola nuts. People who were opposed to alcoholic drinks loved the new coca beverage, although they probably didn't know why it made them feel so good. In 1890, when the state of Georgia prohibited the use of cocaine without a prescription, the Coca-Cola company removed the cocaine from the coca leaves before it used them to flavor the drink. But the name stuck, and so did Coca-Cola's popularity and flavoring.

Opium, codeine, morphine, and cocaine are still important ingredients in painkillers, anesthetics, and other essential medications. Unfortunately, they are also misused, and people who look to these drugs for joy often find that they bring sorrow instead.

3 BILIOUS PILLS AND HUMBUG OIL

When George Washington died in 1799, he was 67 years old. That was considered a ripe old age in those days, but Washington might have lived longer had it not been for the drastic treatments ordered by his doctors. On Friday evening, December 13, 1799, the former president had chills, a sore throat, and a fever, so his personal physician drew about 14 ounces of blood from Washington's arm. That wasn't unusual; bleeding was a standard practice. But the next morning Washington was no better. Two more doctors were called in, and they ordered two more "copious bleedings," a hot pack called a "blister" on his throat and feet, and two doses of calomel, a strong medication made from mercury. Late that afternoon, Washington was bled once again, for a total loss of four pints of blood, enough to put anyone into shock. Then another dose of calomel was forced down his throat, followed by a tartar emetic to make him vomit, and "vapours of vinegar" were blown into his throat. Twenty-four hours after Washington had felt the first chill, he was dead. But he'd had the best medical care available.

When America was only a collection of colonies, doctors were few and far between. People relied on folk medicines, especially the herb recipes brought from their homelands. Even if a doctor was available, the chances were great that he could do little more than set a broken bone, deliver a baby, or comfort the family until the patient got better or died. Typhus, diphtheria, smallpox, infected wounds, pneumonia, and other common diseases could not be cured.

Doctors in the late 1700s were said to practice "heroic" medicine. Surely it was the patients who needed to be heroes. It took stamina and courage to get through most treatments. Medicine was more art than science. One of the most influential doctors of that time was Benjamin Rush, who taught from 1769 until 1813 at Pennsylvania University, one of only four universities in America that trained doctors at that time. In some ways Rush was a man of liberal ideas.

He had signed the Declaration of Independence, and he campaigned for national universities, free schools, education for women, and humane treatment for the insane. But he was unbending in his theories on medicine.

Rush taught doctors that it was nonsense to believe there were different diseases. In his view, there was only one. He called it "irregular arterial action," caused by "excess excitability of the blood vessels"—in other words, high blood pressure, which could be fixed easily by bleeding. Many patients were bled into unconsciousness or even death. But Rush told his classes, "'Tis a very hard matter to bleed a patient to death." Any fainting, weakness, or convulsions following a bleeding was blamed on the patient's illness.

Dr. Rush also believed that "desperate diseases require desperate remedies." So he taught his students to purge a patient with calomel. He called it "a safe and nearly universal medicine." And for generations doctors followed his advice. Calomel's medical name is mercurous chloride. It is a heavy metal that concentrates in the kidneys and shuts them down. Sometimes doses of calomel were so large that a patient's teeth and jawbones were eaten away by the mercury poisoning. If patients survived, they were seldom ever really healthy again.

Medicine hadn't advanced all that much by 1881, when President John Garfield was shot twice. One bullet grazed his arm, but the other was buried in his back. Doctors probed but couldn't find the bullet. X rays hadn't been invented, but Alexander Graham Bell was called in to "sound" for it with an electrical gadget he'd invented. That didn't work either. The bullet wound became infected, and two months later, 50-year-old President Garfield died from an infection that would be cured easily now.

Dr. Lewis Thomas president emeritus of Memorial Sloan-Kettering Cancer Center says that health care was an "unrelievedly deplorable story," as century after century, "medicine got along by sheer guesswork." Nobody knew the cause of any disease. One of the first breakthroughs was the surprising discovery that some diseases run their course and the patient gets better. But patients expected foul-tasting medicine or drastic bleeding, and doctors didn't let them down. If the patient died, the death was blamed on the disease, seldom on the treatment.

Patent Medicines

No wonder people mixed their own medicines or turned to sugar-coated pills and pleasant-tasting patent medicines like Humbug Oil and Lydia Pinkham's Vegetable Compound. The name *patent* medicine came from a practice in England, when a royal letter of patent from the king protected a manufacturer from competition, if he could afford the royal fee. In 1624, British patents by royal favor were outlawed, but the word hung on. Patent medicines did not have to be safe or effective; they had only to be new inventions. In America, patents were issued on the shape of the bottle or container and not on the content of the medicines or the way the ingredients were mixed. The labels and trademarks were copyrighted, and so were the promotional pamphlets wrapped around the product.

Judge Oliver Wendell Holmes called patent medicine makers "toadstool millionaires" because they were greedy and dishonest and their businesses could spring up overnight. Yet people bought millions of bottles of patent drugs rather than go to doctors. The first pills,

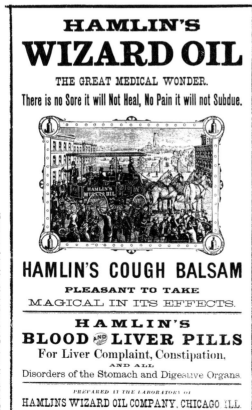

[Courtesy of the New-York Historical Society, New York City]

Hamlin's Wizard Oil was advertised as a magical, pleasant-tasting medical wonder.

poultices, tinctures, and other patent remedies were imported from England and sold in grocery stores, post offices, barbershops, bookstores, and pharmacies.

The first American patent medicine was a product called Bilious Pills, a "cure" for a variety of diseases including yellow fever, jaundice, dysentery, dropsy, and worms. Another was William Swain's Panacea, which sold for three dollars a bottle, a high price in those days, but a bargain if the buyer believed in the promised cure for cancer, rheumatism, hepatitis, gout, and the early stages of syphilis. Panacea was made from sarsaparilla, oil of wintergreen, and mercury.

People bought Carter's Smart Weed, Extract of Wahoo, Belladonna Backache Plasters, and Merchant's Celebrated Gargling Oil for Man and Beast. Anyone with a bit of imagination could make a living by mixing some new nostrum and promising a cure. (A nostrum is a

This poster for Parr English Pad promised a certain and safe cure for all contagious diseases.

(Courtesy of the New-York Historical Society, New York City)

patent medicine or a medicine made by the person who recommends it.) The self-made druggist had only to mix some powder into pills or bottle some liquid, usually with enough alcohol or opium to make it habit-forming, and then make up a dramatic legend to go with it. Cunard's Mountain Herb Pills were sold for decades, along with Dr. Cunard's lurid account of his hair-raising rescue of an Aztec princess who rewarded him with her secret formula for the amazing herb pills.

The label of Clicknor's Purgative Pills assured the buyer that the pills were "completely enveloped with a COATING OF PURE WHITE SUGAR (which is as distinct from the internal ingredients as a nut shell from the kernal) HAVE NO TASTE OF MEDICINE."

Patent medicines sold because they made people feel better. And why not? Hofstetter's Bitters, for example, were 64 percent water and 32 percent alcohol. There was so much opium in some mixtures that a patient was lulled into a false feeling of health while he or she was becoming addicted. It wasn't at all unusual for conservative elderly ladies, "each one of them a pillar of the church and an uncompromising foe of liquor," to find comfort in their favorite patent medicines, which were heavily laced with alcohol or opium.

Many people heard of the germ theory of disease for the first time when they read ads for the Microbe Killer made by William Radam. (This was Louis Pasteur's theory that germs, and not evil spirits, caused disease.) Radam was a gardener who decided that killing microbes in the human body was the same as killing bugs on plants. He advertised that he could "bring all disease under absolute control." His Microbe Killer, patented in 1886, was advertised as "a new and Improved Fumigating Compound for Preserving and Purifying Purposes."

By 1890, Radam's brochures were warning that "to delay for the sake of diagnosis is simply to waste valuable time. It is one of the errors of so-called scientific medicine, and should have nothing to do with the cure." Given that advice, people were all too happy to save the price of a visit to the doctor for a diagnosis, when all they had to do was buy the medicine.

Dr. Howard's Blood Builder Pills came with instructions for patients to get fresh air and adequate sleep and to bathe regularly, which might have kept them healthy even without the pills. Not all patent medicines were soothing and gentle. "Carlton's Nerve and Bone Liniment" was made originally for horses before it was sold for human use. It consisted of turpentine, linseed oil, hemlock, and ammonia. Some all-purpose pills were sold with instructions to give "one for man, two for horse."

Patent medicine makers were the first big-time merchandisers. They were the first to find national markets, the first to help the merchants who retailed their wares, and the first to use clever advertising in newspapers and on billboards. Anyone could advertise anything anywhere. There were no guidelines or ethics. The biggest source of income for many small-town newspapers was patent medicine advertising. Horace Greeley's *New York Tribune* would not accept ads for venereal disease cures or for abortionists, but it allowed ads for just about anything else, from horehound candy that was "good for spitting of blood and contracting of lungs," to "Indian" remedies for cancer, consumption, or falling of the womb.

Lydia Pinkham's products were among the most famous of all patent medicines. The company spent a million dollars a year advertising Lydia Pinkham's Vegetable Compound, at a time when the average wage was five dollars a week. It's been said that Lydia Pinkham's was the most well-known face in America, and more than once a newspaper used her portrait as a stand-in when they needed a picture of Queen Victoria.

Anything advertised as an Indian remedy was successful for the patent medicine makers, including this compound for "coughs, colds, and all affections of the throat and lungs."

(Courtesy of the New-York Historical Society, New York City)

During the Civil War, patent medicine ads took on a military tone. Who could keep from following these "general orders" issued by Dr. Judson, "Adjutant-General," from his "Headquarters"?

> *Pursuant to Division and Brigade orders issued by 8,000 Field Officers, "On the Spot," where they are stationed. All Skedadlers, Deserters, Skulkers, and all others—sick, wounded and cripples— who have foresaken the cause of General Health, shall immediately report to one of the aforesaid officers nearest the point where the delinquent may be at the time this order is made known to him, and purchase one box of*
>

> JUDSON'S
> MOUNTAIN HERB PILLS
>
> *and pay the regulation price therefor. All who comply with the terms of this order, will receive a free pardon for past offences, and be restored to the Grand Army of General Health.*

It was signed by "A. Good Health, Lieutenant-General."

People may have responded to the ad partly because it looked official and partly because the vast majority of people couldn't read very well, if at all. Patent medicine salesmen crisscrossed the nation by horseback, train or wagon, stopping in every crossroad town and village to preach the virtues of their newest wonder drugs. Medicine shows, often with a cast of Indians, sold "snake oil" and dozens of other cures.

Even drugstores sold patent medicines, and often filled their windows with the newest products that promised not only health, but beauty as well.

Early in the 1800s, people went to apothecary shops or pharmacies for medical advice as often as they went to doctors. In Britain, the apothecary shop owners were members of the Grocer's Company before they formed their own guild in open competition with doctors. But in early America, there was little difference between a physician and a druggist. Most doctors bought raw materials from a wholesale druggist and mixed their own compounds. If people couldn't find a doctor or a druggist, they could buy patent medicines at the general store, along with quinine, codeine, opium, and cocaine.

The Move Toward Science

By 1820 a few colleges were beginning to train pharmacists, and the companies that supplied raw materials to druggists were beginning to direct their advertising to doctors instead of to patients. Pharmaceutical makers found that if they emphasized the scientific background of their products, they could not only educate doctors but could urge them to write prescriptions for specific drugs as well.

Dr. Pierce's Favorite Prescriptions were big business in Buffalo, New York, where their "World's Dispensary" was located in the early 1900s.

(Buffalo and Erie County Historical Society)

During the Civil War, when ether and quinine were essential, doctors in battlefield hospitals found that they could not depend on these products to work consistently. One batch might be stronger or weaker than another, and often a batch was contaminated. After the war, a list of standard drugs, called a *pharmacopoeia,* was printed for the first time in the United States.

There was a major change away from the heroic therapies. No longer did pharmacists dispense large doses of basic medicines; they began to fill careful prescriptions for drugs that were aimed at curing specific disorders. A pill machine was invented that could turn out uniform pills faster than they could be rolled by hand. In 1872, the Eureka Sugar Coating Pill Machine made better-tasting pills. But most of these early pills were so hard-packed that they would pass through the body almost as they went in, with the medicines unused.

That changed when Dr. W. E. Upjohn, in Kalamazoo, Michigan, made a "friable" pill that would break apart easily. In October 1884, Upjohn applied for a patent on his process, and by 1886, he and his brothers were in the pill-making business as the Upjohn Pill and Granule Company, which is now the Upjohn Company.

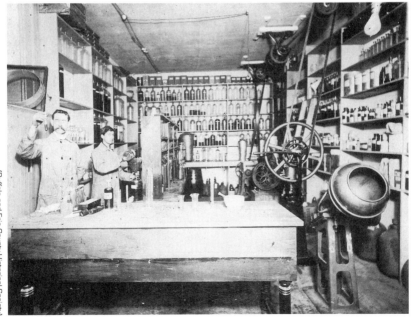

(Buffalo and Erie County Historical Society)

The preparation room of a pharmacy in the early 1900s used the most modern equipment available, including the tumbling machine for rolling pills seen at the far right.

Eli Lilly & Co. opened in 1876, to sell the usual extracts, elixirs, and pills. Three years later, its founder, Colonel Lilly, found a way to make pills easier to swallow and digest by coating them with gelatin.

The First Laws to Regulate Drugs

Gradually, scientists, doctors, and pharmacists began urging the government to establish some kind of control over the production and sale of drugs to eliminate the fly-by-night and unscrupulous medicine maker. In 1902, Congress passed the first law that required manufacturers to be licensed by the secretary of the treasury through the Laboratory of Hygiene. After that, each package of vaccine, serum, or toxin had to be properly labeled and dated, and each company had to agree to "reasonable inspection" of its property at any time.

Congress passed another law in 1906. This one mainly regulated the production of food, but it also had some rules for drugs, especially patent medicines. Under the new rules, inspectors could obtain mail-order patent medicines from the Post Office Department, especially crude drugs, cod liver oil, chemical reagents, and medicinal oils, and check them for arsenic and other contaminants.

(The Upjohn Company)

In 1905, liquid raw materials called fluid extracts were distilled and percolated in rooms like this.

The most important result of the 1906 act was the reduction of alcohol and narcotics in patent medicines. Hofstetter's Bitters, for example, had contained 32 percent alcohol, and under the new law the alcohol content dropped to 25 percent. The first case brought by the government under this law was against Harper's CUFORHEDAKE BRANEFUDE, which was found guilty of mislabeling. The company did not tell buyers that its headache cure was mostly alcohol, mixed with some coal tar. The jury in the case was charged only with deciding whether or not the label was misleading, and they voted the company guilty of calling its product "brain food."

Of the first thousand prosecutions under the 1906 Act, 376 were against drugs that made exaggerated claims to cure everything from blood disorders to insomnia, and drugs that were impure or contained unidentified compounds. Humbug Oil claimed to cure diphtheria. When government prosecutors found it was made from 60 percent alcoholic ammonia and codeine and 40 percent turpentine and linseed oil, they ordered Humbug Oil off the market. The manufacturer was fined only five dollars, but at least no one could buy the drug.

Medicine moved into a new era as basic science research discovered the causes of diseases and created the drugs to fight them. But a gap

(The Upjohn Company)

This was the packaging and labeling department of the Upjohn Company in 1910. Today, all pharmaceutical products are packaged on automated assembly lines.

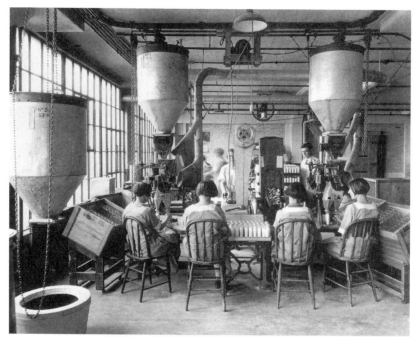

(The Upjohn Company)

This was a "sterile" filling line at the Upjohn Company in the 1930s.

remained between professional pharmacists and the drug companies. It was as though trained pharmacists couldn't let go of the old image of drug makers as snake-oil salesmen. As recently as 1927, the American Society of Pharmacology and Experimental Therapeutics had a rule for its members: "Entrance into the permanent employ of a drug firm shall constitute forfeiture of membership."

But when the manufacturers also became involved in research and became the discoverers as well as the makers of drugs, attitudes changed, and the stage was set for some near-miracles in the pharmaceutical industry.

4 THE MAGIC BULLET

In January 1917, while the world waited to see if the United States would go to war with Germany, the U-boat *Deutschland* was docked in New York harbor. The German submarine's cargo was Salvarsan, a drug also known as 606 and the "magic bullet." Eight years earlier, a German bacteriologist, Paul Ehrlich, had developed Salvarsan as the first effective medicine against syphilis. Syphilis is spread by sexual contact and by an infected mother to her unborn child. Left untreated, syphilis causes brain damage and, eventually, death. It had been a devastating, uncontrolled social disease for centuries, as frightening then as AIDS is now. Both the Germans and the Americans knew that during wartime syphilis would spread rapidly and that the chemotherapy of Salvarsan would be essential.

We tend to think of chemotherapy as a modern technique, a new breakthrough in treating cancer, for example, but Paul Ehrlich coined the word more than a hundred years ago. Chemotherapy is the treatment of disease with chemical compounds. The compounds may come from plants, from animal venom or hormones, or from microorganisms such as bacteria or fungi, or they may be synthesized from raw chemicals.

Science usually moves ahead in small steps, but Ehrlich's "magic bullet" was a giant step. Like all scientists, Ehrlich built on the research of scientists before him. In the 1860s, Louis Pasteur had announced his germ theory of disease. This incredibly important medical discovery convinced people that infections and diseases were caused by tiny microorganisms, not by evil spirits.

When the English surgeon Joseph Lister heard of Pasteur's work, he was determined to try to wipe out the germs that caused infections and killed patients after surgery even when the operation itself was successful. Lister sprayed the air in his operating room and washed his surgical instruments with an antiseptic called carbolic acid. He insisted on surgical gloves or at least washed hands and clean aprons for anyone assisting in surgery. Lister allowed no surgeon to appear wearing bloody clothes loaded with germs from previous operations, or to use the same set of unsterilized instruments on one patient after another.

Then German bacteriologist Robert Koch took several big scientific steps when he learned to cultivate bacteria outside a living body, and that allowed him to follow the entire life cycle of an organism. At first he used blood serum to nurture the bacteria, but then he developed a gelatin, made from seaweed, called agar-agar. He added nutrient broth for the bacteria to feed on. His assistant, Julius Petri, made covered shallow glass dishes to hold the agar, and they worked so well that petri dishes have been used in labs ever since.

Koch set the rules that everyone would follow from then on for identifying disease-causing bacteria. First, the microorganism must be found in a diseased animal. Then it must live in a culture outside the animal. When it is put into a healthy animal, the microorganism must cause the suspected disease. And last, the same kind of bacteria found in the original diseased animal must be found in the newly diseased animal. Using these rules, Koch identified the bacteria that cause two of the world's deadliest diseases, tuberculosis and cholera.

Cells are transparent and difficult to see under a microscope. Biologists had found that if they stained cells with the newly discovered aniline dyes made from coal tar, they were easier to identify. The dyes killed the cells, but that's what led to the discovery of Salvarsan.

At a meeting in Berlin in 1882, Dr. Paul Ehrlich heard Robert Koch tell how he used dye to discover the tuberculosis bacillus. Ehrlich had worked with dyes when he was a college student, but Koch's work renewed his interest, and he rushed home to try some experiments of his own. He worked late into the night, staining some slides of sputum taken from patients with tuberculosis. The iron stove in his lab had gone out, and he placed the slides on the cold stove to dry overnight.

The next morning Ehrlich returned to his lab to find that the maid had started a fire in the stove. He was furious. He grabbed the warmed slides, certain that they were ruined. But when he held them up against the light, he found that they were beautifully stained. The tuberculosis bacteria stood out in clumps that were unmistakable. The warmth of the stove had helped the process of staining.

Ehrlich showed his slides to Dr. Koch, who recognized the importance of this accidental discovery. Later he wrote:

> *. . . with Ehrlich's method of staining, the recognition of the tuber-*
> *cule bacilli could readily be made use of in diagnosis. We owe it to*
> *this circumstance alone that it has become a general custom to*
> *search for the bacillus in sputum, whereas, without it, it is likely*
> *that but few investigators would have concerned themselves with*
> *tubercule bacilli.*

Ehrlich was a great believer in what he called his big "G's, *Geduld, Gelt, und Gluck,*" or patience, money, and luck.

When Ehrlich found that methylene blue dye stained only nerve tissue and left the surrounding tissue unstained, it gave him an idea. If only the nerve tissue was affected by the dye, maybe the dye could be used to deaden nerve cells to relieve pain without damaging any other cells. He tried it; he gave methylene blue to patients with severe arthritis, and it did relieve their pain. But he had to stop the experiment because long-term use of the dye caused kidney damage. When Ehrlich stained other organisms with methylene blue, he found that the dye killed the organism that causes malaria. In 1891, he gave the dye to two malaria patients and they were cured. But they had only a mild form of the disease. In later trials, Ehrlich found that quinine was still better than dye for more severe cases of malaria. It wasn't a defeat for Ehrlich but actually a major breakthrough, because it was the first time a synthetic drug had killed a specific disease organism. And it gave Ehrlich the determination to find a "magic bullet," a drug that would search out and destroy a specific disease organism without hurting other cells.

Next Ehrlich turned his attention to sleeping sickness because it was so widespread in tropical countries that there were fears it might wipe out half the population of Africa. He knew that sleeping sickness was caused by a protozoan called trypanosome that was carried by the tsetse fly. He also knew that an arsenic compound called atoxol had some slight effect on this trypanosome. So Ehrlich started his search by asking his laboratory assistants to make similar compounds. He figured that by using atoxol as a starting point, he was at least heading in the right direction.

Ehrlich and his assistants tested hundreds of substances, but even when he found no magic bullet to kill off sleeping sickness, he did not stop. Ehrlich was a tireless worker. Every morning he was up early, eating his breakfast in his study while he made plans for himself and his assistants. Each of his researchers would get Ehrlich's assignment for the day, written on colored paper, with the methods and lab techniques given in detail. He called the colored sheets of instructions his laboratory blocks, and he expected the work to be done precisely as written.

Ehrlich's work may have been precise, but his study was a mess. Manuscripts, books, magazines, and notes were piled along the walls, on every chair, on the writing desk next to the window, and covering the big table in the center of the room. Only narrow pathways allowed him to walk through the piles of papers littering the floor. Ehrlich had warned his cleaning lady not to rearrange any of these piles. He told her that he had put poison between the books and papers and that she could die if she touched anything. (Of course, he hadn't!)

Ehrlich's personal lab was as unusual as his study. An immense laboratory table that almost filled the room was covered with all sizes and shapes of bottles of chemicals he was testing. They were arranged in a system that only he knew, and he could always find what he wanted. The only other equipment on the table was a single bunsen burner, a microscope, a small box of slides, and a wooden box of test tubes. Shelves along the walls held the usual reagents and chemicals used to make most solutions, but the chemist's usual flasks, graduates, and other glassware were missing. Ehrlich worked only with slides and test tubes.

The Cure for Syphilis

In 1906 Ehrlich heard from another researcher that the sleeping sickness trypanosome was in many ways similar to the long, thin spiral organism called a spirochete that causes syphilis. Mercury compounds had been used to treat syphilis, but they had very little effect on the spirochete and often had major side effects for the patient. Ehrlich decided to try the same arsenic compounds he'd aimed at the sleeping sickness trypanosome on the syphilis spirochete. His biggest problem was finding an animal to test in on.

Mice did not get syphilis. However, Ehrlich knew of a scientist in Tokyo, Sacachiro Hata, who had found a way of infecting rabbits with syphilis. In 1909, when Hata joined Ehrlich's lab in Germany, Ehrlich gave him all the compounds that he and his assistants had put together in the past three years. One by one, Hata tested the compounds in dozens of different combinations. When he came to number 606, an arsenic compound, he found that it killed the syphilis spirochete in rabbits. It was an exciting moment, but no one celebrated because it still had to be tested on humans.

After several hundred syphilis patients had been treated with 606, Ehrlich knew that they had found the magic bullet. He named it Salvarsan, which comes from Greek, meaning "saved by arsenic."

Salvarsan was a harsh, painful treatment for patients, often lasting a year or more. But considering the outcome of syphilis, most patients willingly suffered through the Salvarsan injections rather than let the disease destroy them.

Because Salvarsan contains the potent poison arsenic, Ehrlich worried about its dangerous side effects. He insisted that the new drug be given only to the most seriously ill patients, and that doctors report the results back to him, especially when they found toxic effects. Ehrlich was not at ease until a large sample of patients had been tested. In 1910, a drug manufacturer agreed to supply 65,000 doses of Salvarsan at no cost to doctors or patients. Although the drug company kept careful records of all its shipments, Ehrlich kept his own records. Every day he wrote down the number of doses, the strength of each dose, the date it was given, the doctor's name, and the name of the hospital or clinic—but he didn't write in a notebook. He listed the data on the insides of the doors of his bookcases! His secretary recalled that often she would find Ehrlich sitting on his heels before an open cupboard door, adding to his list the number of dosages sent that week. He followed that up by writing to each doctor, asking for

(National Library of Medicine)

Paul Ehrlich is famous for his discovery of a "magic bullet" medicine that targeted the disease syphilis.

their own observations of each patient. His sense of responsibility for this drug was so great that he followed up on every undesirable report.

Salvarsan was a complex drug to manufacture, and things could go wrong at any stage. Ehrlich insisted on having a sample of each batch of the drug sent to his laboratory so it could be tested for impurities. That's how he discovered the importance of using Salvarsan while it was fresh. It was necessary to keep the drug sealed and away from the air. Aging and oxidation (mixing with air) destroyed the purity of the drug. Ehrlich's close control over the production and distribution of the drug and careful monitoring of its effectiveness became a model that the pharmaceutical industry follows today.

Paul Ehrlich's secretary, Marthe Marquart, wrote,

> *No outsider can realize the amount of work involved in those long hours of experiments that had to be repeated and repeated for months on end. People often refer to 606 as the 606th experiment; this is not correct, for 606 is the number of the substance with which, with all the previous ones, very numerous experiments were made. The amount of work which all of this involved is beyond imagination.*

Drugs are chemicals, and they can react only with other chemicals. On the membrane of each cell there are chemicals that react with or receive other chemicals. The spot on the membrane where one chemical receives another is called the receptor site. As Paul Ehrlich described the action, it was almost as though the cell had arms that reached out and grabbed the right chemical. In order for a drug to work, it must have the right chemical makeup to fit the receptor site on the bacterium or other disease organism. At the same time, that drug's structure must not fit receptor sites in the patient's cells because that would cause harmful side effects.

Many of the basic techniques of chemotherapy come directly from Paul Ehrlich's work on malaria, sleeping sickness, and syphilis. His idea of starting with a compound that has some—maybe only slight—but some effect on a disease organism is still used when biochemists search for a new drug. The chemicals they use may be synthetic, or they may come from plant poisons or animal venom or hormones. With one of these as a model, chemists can synthesize hundreds, even thousands, of closely related chemicals until they find one with the right structure to fit the receptor site. That's what a magic bullet means in chemotherapy—a direct hit from one chemical compound to the receptor site of the disease organism.

After Ehrlich's success, every lab geared up to find other magic bullets. From then on, every sick person expected to be cured with a magic bullet kind of medicine. But the future held bigger surprises. There were near-miracles ahead in the drug industry, and there were many disappointments.

5 THE SULFA DRUGS

After Ehrlich's attack on syphilis, every laboratory in the world started testing dyes and other chemicals to find miracle drugs. What was needed most was a drug that would cure general bacterial infections. Often, operations were successful, but patients died from an infection afterwards. Blood poisoning or septicemia could rage through the body after a simple pinprick or scratch. Puerperal fever, more commonly called childbed fever, killed one out of every 500 women after the birth of a baby.

The I. G. Farben Company in Germany was determined to be one of the leaders in finding new drugs, and they hired Dr. Gerhard Domagk as the director of their new experimental pathology laboratory. The Farben company tested experimental drugs on a strain of mice that had been infected with a particularly virulent strain of streptococcus bacteria, the organism that causes blood poisoning. These bacteria killed the infected mice in four days. Dr. Domagk knew that only a powerful drug could save the mice—or people—infected with the bacteria.

Like Ehrlich, Domagk started by testing chemicals that had shown some success against the disease he was after. One of these was a gold compound. It did kill the streptococcus bacteria in mice, but it caused serious kidney and liver damage when it was used in humans.

Next Domagk turned to a new orange-red dye with the trade name of Prontosil. When infected mice were injected with Prontosil, they all survived. But before Dr. Domagk had a chance to begin testing Prontosil on humans, he got a call from a doctor asking if Domagk knew of anything that might save the life of a 10-month-old baby boy who was dying from staphyloccal blood poisoning. The doctor was so desperate that Domagk gave him some of the Prontosil tablets. But he warned the doctor that as far as he knew, Prontosil only worked against the streptococcal blood poisoning. It had not been tried on a staph infection.

The doctor gave Prontosil to the baby because there was little choice. After four days, the baby's temperature was down, and he was feeling better. Within three weeks, the baby was cured and sent home from the hospital. It was the first successful use of Prontosil.

Not long after, Domagk published a paper giving the complete experimental results of the new drug. He expected that doctors would clamor for it and demand Prontosil immediately, but they didn't. Despite the amazing cure of the baby, doctors paid no attention to Prontosil. They had accepted Ehrlich's drug, which worked against protozoa and spirochetes, but they seemed to think that no chemical could work against a wide range of smaller bacteria. Then a dramatic incident convinced them.

On October 3, 1935, Leonard Colebrook was in the audience at a meeting of the Royal Society of Medicine in London, when Dr. Domagk gave a lecture about Prontosil. Colebrook was a doctor at

Dr. Gerhard Domagk discovered Prontosil, a drug that killed streptococcus bacteria in the human body. The active ingredient was sulfanilamide, the first of the fabulous sulfa drugs.

(National Library of Medicine)

Queen Charlotte's Maternity Hospital, where childbed fever was as common as in any other hospital. Colebrook became so excited about Prontosil that he immediately ordered a supply and started clinical trials at his hospital. He treated 26 seriously ill women with the drug, and all of them got well. There was no better evidence that a drug could cure a general bacterial infection.

The First Sulfa Drug

Meanwhile, at the Pasteur Institute in France, Dr. Daniele Bovet was puzzled by a peculiar characteristic of Prontosil. The drug worked against streptococcus bacteria in the human body, but it did not work against the same bacteria in a test tube. The only reason Bovet could imagine for this was that Prontosil was broken down in the body, and that only part of the drug was the active agent that killed the bacteria. Bovet's experiments soon proved he was right. The active part of Prontosil turned out to be a colorless substance he called sulfanil-amide.

Then another strange event occurred, which brought this sulfa drug to the public's attention. In 1936, Franklin Roosevelt, Jr., the son of the president of the United States, was dying from severe blood poisoning. The president's wife Eleanor had heard of the new sulfa drug. When she appealed for help, the drug was airmailed from Germany, and it saved her son's life. Not many years earlier, President Coolidge's son had died from a similar infection because there was no effective medicine.

In 1939, when the Nobel Prize committee in Sweden announced that Gerhard Domagk would be honored for his discovery, the German Gestapo, or secret police, arrested him. Domagk was jailed for a week while the Gestapo "convinced" him not to accept the award from one of the country's enemy nations. After World War II, Dr. Domagk went to Stockholm to receive his belated prize, but it must have seemed like an anticlimax because he had already had the best of all rewards. In February of 1935, Domagk's daughter, Hildegard, had pricked her finger with a needle. It became infected, and blood poisoning raged through her body—but large injections of Prontosil killed the infection, and she recovered.

After Bovet's discovery of the active ingredient in Prontosil, more than 5,000 different sulfa drugs were made and tested. Only about 15 of these new sulfas proved to be of real value. But during World War II, every first aid kit issued to soldiers contained packets of sulfa powder that could be used on battlefield wounds. Those packets probably saved hundreds of thousands of lives.

A Deadly Sulfa Drug

In 1937, an American pharmaceutical company wanted to make a liquid sulfa drug they called Elixir of Sulphanilamide. In order to make the drug soluble for injections, it was mixed with diethylene glycol, which is the same chemical now used for antifreeze in cars. During the two months the Elixir was on the market, 76 people died from severe kidney and liver damage. But some good did come from the tragedy. Congress passed the Food and Drug Act. This act was the beginning of the Food and Drug Administration (FDA), the organization that protects the consumer by approving or disapproving every drug before it can be sold in the United States.

6 PENICILLIN, THE WONDER DRUG

If Alexander Fleming had tested penicillin on sick animals instead of healthy ones, the miraculous mold might have become a drug 10 years earlier. Fleming's discovery of penicillin has been called an accident, but the great scientist Louis Pasteur would have disagreed. He said that luck favors the prepared mind. In other words, you have to know what you're looking for when an "accident" shows up, and Fleming knew. But it certainly was a case of serendipity.

The mold's name comes from the Latin word *penicillus,* which means brush. Seen under a microscope, branches of penicillin mold look like small brushes. Like all members of the fungus family, *Penicillium* reproduces with spores, which are like primitive seeds. Seeds result when a flower is fertilized—a combining of male and female cells. Spores are asexual. They need no male and female parts. Spores float in the air and grow wherever they find a moist, warm surface. Researchers hate them. Every time a test tube or petri dish is opened in a laboratory, there's a chance that mold spores can contaminate the experiment.

Sir Alexander Fleming had served in Britain's Royal Army Medical Corps during World War I, and this made him very aware of the need for better antiseptics. Shrapnel from exploding mines and gunshot wounds caused terrible infections that were almost impossible to cure. After the war, Fleming went to work in the inoculation department of St. Mary's Hospital in London. In 1921, he found a mysterious substance in mucus that kills bacteria. When he experimented further, he discovered that this substance was a protein that occurs naturally in tears and saliva and on nails, skin, and other tissue. He called it lysozyme. *Lyso* is from the Greek word that means dissolve, and *zyme* from the Greek word meaning to mix. For six years he worked on

Greatly enlarged under a microscope, filaments of the miracle mold Penicillin notatum *look like little dust brushes.*

(Paul Facklam)

lysozymes, but he never found a way to purify them or to use them to treat infectious diseases.

After the discovery of the sulfa drugs, researchers everywhere were hoping to find other chemicals to target diseases, especially the surface infections that could be so deadly. So when Fleming found penicillin, he saw it as a way to treat infected surface wounds, but not as a general medicine that would attack infections inside the body.

The Discovery

One day in 1928, Dr. Fleming was cleaning up his lab, and as he always did, he checked each petri dish before he threw the contents away. On one agar plate he found large yellow colonies of mold growing over a culture of bacteria. Fleming had been studying the staphylococcus, which is a common bacterium on skin and produces pus in an infection. This particular culture had come from the boils of a patient at the hospital. The mold was not the kind found commonly on bread or cheese, but a rarer relative known as *Penicillin notatum*.

Around the blob of mold that had ruined the bacteria culture, Fleming saw a wide, clear area where the staphylococci were disappearing. Where other colonies of bacteria were dissolving, the yellow mold was turning to liquid. It looked like drops of water. Fleming could see that something was killing the harmful bacteria. He had the culture photographed for his records before he started to experiment. Wherever he spread the yellow mold juice on sterile agar plates, bacteria were stopped dead. Bacteria would grow right up to the edge of the mold juice, then disappear. Even when it was highly diluted, the penicillin juice killed bacteria.

Fleming named his new antiseptic penicillin. He injected it into a healthy rabbit and a mouse, with no harm to either animal, but he did not inject it into sick animals. The chairman of the inoculation department, Sir Almroth Wright, did not believe that experimenting on live animals with infectious material had any relation to treating sick people, and Fleming followed his wishes. Had he tried the penicillin on infected animals, Fleming would have seen its power. However, he did want to know if this germ-killer would be harmful to people.

When he mixed the mold-juice with human blood, the penicillin did not kill off the white cells, which are the infection fighters in the body's immune system. That was a good sign. Then Fleming used some of the penicillin solution to wash out an infected eye of one of his lab assistants, and the infection cleared up.

Next he had to find out if this new antiseptic could be purified. Fleming gave the yellow mold juice to two young lab assistants, Stuart Graddock and Frederick Riley. First, they discovered that the yellow color was only an impurity. When they tried to separate pure penicillin from the rest of the solution, they ended up with a brown, sticky goop that looked like melted toffee candy.

Even without pure penicillin crystals, Fleming decided he was ready to present his discovery to other scientists. On February 13, 1929, he read his paper on penicillin at a meeting of the Medical Research Club. He wasn't a very forceful speaker, and there was no response from the audience when he finished. No one asked a question or made a comment. Fleming must have been disappointed, because he had done what was expected of all good scientists. He had kept careful notes and reported the details of the experiments. After his talk, he filed his notes on penicillin and turned again to his work on lysozymes, although he did continue to use penicillin to get rid of unwanted bacteria that grew on cultures in his lab. A dozen years went by before other scientists turned his discovery into a powerful antibiotic.

Many people have speculated on why Fleming didn't develop penicillin into a workable drug, but Dr. Gladys Hobby has made an

Sir Alexander Fleming discovered penicillin in 1928 and identified its amazing ability to destroy bacteria without harming other tissue.

[National Library of Medicine]

interesting comment. She was one of three American scientists at Columbia University who also worked on penicillin. "Each of us starts with a simple observation, perhaps even a 'discovery,' and all else follows," she wrote. "One person after another builds on the original observation, ultimately bringing scientific advancement and success. Each does what is possible in his time. Had Fleming not made the observation and preserved the culture, had he not demonstrated the presence of penicillin in his culture fluids and recorded its properties, there would have been no starting point for Chain and Florey's studies 10 years later."

The Wonder Drug

Howard Walter Florey, a young Australian doctor, was chief of the Sir William Dunn School of Pathology in Oxford, England in 1938. He, too, was studying lysozymes, in search of any natural substance that would kill bacteria without harming other cells. Like Fleming, he didn't have enough knowledge of chemistry to purify the lysozymes, so he hired a biochemist, 29-year-old Dr. Ernst Boris Chain, who had fled from Hitler-controlled Germany. Florey also hired Dr. Norman G. Heatley, who was well known for his ability to invent instruments and techniques for working with microscopic organisms. These three men became the penicillin team.

Florey had been searching through scientific papers for anything on natural substances that kill bacteria when he came across Fleming's brief paper. Mold juice? He wondered, could it really work? Could it be another great drug like the sulfanilamides?

Florey got a sample of Fleming's penicillin mold and put his team to work on it. Dr. Chain was in charge of growing the mold and trying to purify it, while Florey tried to figure out how it worked, and Heatley created the right equipment. England was gearing up for war in 1938, and it was not a good time to start a major research project. Money was needed for ammunition and troops—not for science. But Florey's team went ahead because they knew that if they could make a workable drug from penicillin, it could save countless lives on the battlefield.

Howard Walter Florey headed the team that turned Fleming's discovery into a wonder drug in time to save countless lives during World War II.

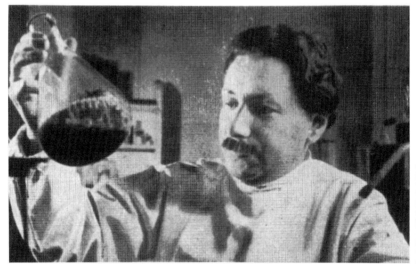

Biochemist Dr. Ernst Boris Chain was only 29 years old when Dr. Florey hired him as part of the penicillin team.

(National Library of Medicine)

First they found that penicillin mold grew faster if they added brewer's yeast to the broth. But when Dr. Chain tried to separate the penicillin from the juice created by the mold, it kept disappearing. Finally Heatley used ether to extract penicillin from the juice, and water to remove the penicillin from the ether. When the experimenters learned that the penicillin had to be kept cold, Heatley rigged up a system of glass tubes and coils wrapped in crushed ice. By March 1940, Florey's team had produced pure penicillin. After they freeze-dried the gallons of mold juice they had so carefully collected, there was only a small pile of dry brown powder, barely enough to cover a dime.

They tested penicillin on different bacteria and found that it killed the germs that cause scarlet fever, pneumonia, diphtheria, and meningitis. In contact with penicillin, these microorganisms would swell up and burst. Next they had to test the mold's effectiveness in animals.

On May 25, 1940, they injected eight healthy mice with streptococcus bacteria. Four mice were put back in their cages with no treatment. They were the "control." Of the four other mice, two were injected with just one dose of penicillin. The remaining two mice were given half that dose of penicillin, but the dose was repeated four more times in the next 10 hours. All day and all night, the men watched and kept

(Sir William Dunn School of Pathology, University of Oxford)

The third man on the penicillin team was Dr. Norman G. Heatley, who was especially skilled in the techniques of working with microscopic organisms.

careful notes. By morning, all the mice that had not been treated with penicillin—the control mice—had died from the streptococcus infection. All the mice that had received penicillin, in one dose or in several doses, were alive. The new drug worked—it killed bacteria in living animals and it did not injure the animals. It still had to be tested on humans, but a bigger supply of penicillin was needed for that.

By this time the war was escalating. If Germany invaded England the casualties would be enormous. The research had to go on. Florey and Chain rubbed spores from the penicillin mold into pockets of their suits and the linings of raincoats. They knew the spores would lie dormant indefinitely, and the men hoped that if England were invaded at least one of them could escape to Canada or the United States with the precious mold.

They worked frantically. Could they make enough of the drug in time? Dr. Florey told his team, "Try anything, but get it done as quickly as possible."

They knew that penicillin grew best in shallow dishes where it could get oxygen. Soon every shallow bottle, bowl, and pot they could find became a mold garden. They used pie pans, milk cans, tin trays, china meat platters, rows of gallon-size lemonade bottles with screw tops, a bronze letterbox, milk churns, and even a dog bath. But the containers that worked best were bedpans. Finally Heatley found a factory that would make rectangular, shallow clay pots with lids and side spouts similar in shape to the bedpans. The women hired to work in the ice-cold penicillin fermentation rooms got the nickname "Penicillin Girls." They wore fur-lined boots, and under their lab coats they wore overcoats and scarves as they turned bottles and kept an eye on the growing mold.

On August 24, 1940, the British medical magazine *The Lancet* published Florey's article entitled "Penicillin as a Chemotherapeutic Agent." Dr. Florey listed all seven people who had worked in the lab in alphabetical order, rather than in order of rank as many department heads did. He gave equal credit to each member of the team. Florey was greatly disappointed when not one pharmaceutical company called to ask about the new drug, but he was surprised to hear from Dr. Alexander Fleming. Fleming wanted to see Florey's lab and the production of "my old penicillin." When he arrived, Fleming showed great interest in the process, but he made few comments and did not congratulate these men who had taken his discovery and made it into a working medicine.

The "Penicillin Girls" who tended the shallow ceramic pans of penicillin were an important part of Florey's team that produced quantities of the new antibiotic in 1941.

The First Tests on Sick People

By 1941, Florey and Chain had already tried penicillin on themselves, but now they were ready to test it on sick people. Albert Alexander, a 43-year-old Oxford policeman, was dying. He had scratched his mouth and it was infected with both staphylococcus and streptococcus bacteria. The infection had spread to his bones and lungs. On February 12, 1941, a solution of penicillin was dripped into his veins, but it didn't look as though they'd have enough. Fortunately, penicillin is rapidly excreted in the urine, and Dr. Florey said that the patient's kidneys removed the penicillin so fast that it was "like trying to fill a bath with the plug out." So they collected the urine and took it back to the lab, where the precious penicillin was recycled. Dr. Florey's wife, Ethel, and the others who took turns bicycling back to the lab with the urine were known as the "P-patrol."

In 24 hours, the policeman's fever was down, and in another day or two he was eating and feeling better. But the penicillin supply ran out. Even the penicillin collected from his urine was quickly used up. A month later, Albert Alexander died. As depressed as Florey and Chain were, they knew that penicillin worked—if only they could make enough. But still no manufacturers in England would take on the project. More seriously ill people were treated with the drug, and all of them improved, but they died later because there wasn't enough penicillin to continue treatment. Finally a 14-year-old boy and a six-month-old baby were treated and survived, and the word "miracle" was used in speaking of the new drug.

The American Team

After Florey's report in *The Lancet* in 1940, laboratories in other countries had asked for samples of the penicillin. A team at Columbia University in New York City, Dr. Martin Dawson, Dr. Gladys Hobby, and Dr. Karl Meyer, had made a small amount of penicillin in September 1940, and a month later they gave it to two patients at the Presbyterian Hospital in New York. Describing those penicillin preparations, Dr. Hobby wrote that they were " . . . extremely crude, but highly active." These were the first clinical trials in the United States. Dr. Dawson's team had the same problem as Florey's, however. They needed a way to produce larger amounts of penicillin. Having used every inch of space in their small lab, they began to move the flasks of penicillin in and out of classrooms as the students moved out and in. Finally they found that the penicillin would incubate nicely under the seats of a two-story ampitheater, at least during the eight months when room temperatures were right for the mold to grow.

British pharmaceutical firms couldn't take on the production of penicillin because they were already working to capacity. So Florey decided to ask the Americans for help. He had received a few thousand dollars from the Rockefeller Foundation for research, and he was certain the foundation would help again. So Florey and Heatley packed their briefcases with reports and freeze-dried penicillin mold and flew a long, roundabout secret journey to America by way of Portugal that seemed right out of a spy movie.

Eventually they arrived in Peoria, Illinois, where the U.S. Department of Agriculture had a research lab, and it was there that penicillin got the boost that put it into production. Dr. Robert Coghill, who was the director of the lab, suggested a process used in making beer. It was called "deep fermentation," a method that would grow the mold in huge tanks instead of in shallow dishes. Another researcher, Dr. Andrew Moyer, suggested using corn steep liquor, which is a gooey, sticky waste product from the lab's process of taking starch out of corn. Again serendipity played a part. Florey did not know that this was the only laboratory in the United States where corn steep liquor was routinely tried as a culture medium, and in it, 12 times as much penicillin was produced.

While Heatley stayed in Peoria to learn about the deep vat production, Florey visited drug companies in the United States and Canada. Over and over he repeated the story of penicillin, but not one company was willing to take on the experimental drug. Florey was almost ready to give up. Finally, just 10 days after Japan attacked Pearl Harbor on December 7, 1941, four American drug manufacturers—Merck Sharp & Dohme; Pfizer Company; E. R. Squibb & Sons; and Lederle—decided they were ready to mass-produce penicillin. Drug companies always guard their secrets from one another, but with America at war, they worked together. Everyone knew how desperately the country would need a miracle drug to treat the heavy war casualties, and other drug makers were quick to join in.

Back in England, Florey's group was working tirelessly to make and test penicillin, when a strange event brought Dr. Fleming back into the picture. On August 5, 1942, Fleming called Florey because a close friend of his was desperately sick with streptococcal meningitis. Fleming asked if Florey could send him some penicillin. There was only one bottle to spare in the lab, but how could Florey refuse the person who had discovered it? Florey delivered the penicillin to Fleming himself.

Dr. Fleming injected the drug into his friend, but the man did not improve. Fleming called Florey to ask if he had ever injected penicillin directly into a person's spinal fluid. Florey had not, but he said he'd try it. When Dr. Florey tried it on a cat, the cat died. Immediately, he called Fleming to warn him, but it was too late—Fleming had taken the chance and injected it into his friend's spinal fluid. The man got better so quickly that word spread about the miraculous drug. Reporters picked it up, and it wasn't long before Alexander Fleming was famous.

Even with penicillin in production in the United States, the drug companies kept looking for ways to make it better and faster. All during the war men of the U.S. Army Transport Command were under orders to collect soil samples from India, Africa, South America, and China and send them to Peoria in the hopes that a better strain of mold might show up. Employees of the U.S. Department of Agriculture lab in Peoria also kept their eyes open for mold, but nobody was more enthusiastic about the project than Mary Hunt. As she picked through garbage cans, trash bins, and litter, people began calling her "Moldy Mary." One summer day in 1943, she found a cantaloupe with mold she said had a "pretty golden look." When it was tested in the lab, the cantaloupe mold was perfect. It grew well in the deep tanks, and it yielded more than twice the penicillin that Fleming's original mold had produced. It was given the name *Penicillium chrysogenum*, and after that Fleming's *Penicillium notatum* was no longer used.

By May 1945, when Germany surrendered, penicillin had saved millions of lives. The making of this drug was an incredible example of what could be done when government, industry, and university researchers worked together. America contributed the technique of deep fermentation, the corn steep liquor, the cantaloupe mold, and the first mass production of penicillin, but England was the birthplace of the miraculous drug. In December 1945, Sir Alexander Fleming, Sir Howard Florey, and Dr. Ernst Chain shared the Nobel Prize in medicine.

Today's penicillin is no longer made from mold. In 1957, Dr. John Sheehan at Massachusetts Institute of Technology made the drug entirely from chemicals, and that changed the direction of biomedical research forever.

7 MAIL-IN MOLD

After the discovery of penicillin every research lab was searching for more antibiotics. No one knew how many thousands of different molds and fungi might become medicines.

The Bristol-Meyers Company in Syracuse, New York sent envelopes to all its stockholders with instructions to return samples of soil from their cellars, gardens, and backyards. Other pharmaceutical companies asked for mold samples from missionaries, foreign correspondents, airline pilots, oil and mineral prospectors, deep sea divers, and anyone who traveled around the world.

Chloromycetin

In 1943, in an old laboratory at Yale University, Dr. Paul Burkholder began to collect soil samples. He sent plastic mailing tubes and stamps to people all over the world. Of the 7,000 tubes of soil returned to him, four contained organisms that were unusually active against bacteria. He sent those four samples to the Parke Davis Company in Detroit for further testing. One of the four was spectacular. Living in the soil sample from Venezuela was a fungus that produced chloromycetin. Not only did this new antibiotic kill many different bacteria, but it was also deadly to a tiny organism called rickettsia, which causes Rocky Mountain spotted fever and typhus.

Typhus is an ancient disease carried by lice living on rats. It had caused some of the most tragic epidemics in history, and during World War II it had raged through concentration camps and refugee settlements. In 1947, when Parke Davis had just begun to make chloromycetin, a typhus epidemic broke out in Peru and Bolivia. Dr. Eugene Payne flew to South America with all the chloromycetin Parke Davis had— enough to treat 22 people.

He had no choice but to take care of only the most desperately ill patients. Patient No. 10, Gregorio Zalles, had been in a coma for three days. His death certificate had even been filled in, except for the date. Forty minutes after Dr. Payne injected the chloromycetin, Zalles asked for a glass of water. Zalles and the 21 other patients recovered. After this first use on humans, chloromycetin was hailed as the greatest drug since penicillin.

Aureomycin

At the Lederle Company laboratories, a retired botany professor, Dr. Benjamin Duggar, tested samples of soil sent to him by friends at universities around the country. One day in 1944, he opened a small bottle of dirt labeled "Sample 67: Columbia, MO. Plot #23. Timothy field, no fertilization. Silt loam. Sanborn Field. University of Missouri." In it he found an unknown species of fungus, which he recorded as Actinomycetes A-377. The fungus didn't appear to be especially active against bacteria in the first tests, and it was suggested to Dr. Duggar that he ought to drop it and move on to more promising samples. But Dr. Duggar kept testing, and eventually he found that the fungus produced a substance that killed bacteria that were unaffected by either penicillin or a newer antibiotic, streptomycin.

As an added benefit, A-377 also killed the spotted fever rickettsia. Duggar called the new antibiotic aureomycin. In its first clinical trial, aureomycin saved a boy who was in a coma from Rocky Mountain spotted fever. It also saved several patients with such severe cases of syphilis that the bacteria had become immune to salvarsan and penicillin. But the real glory or aureomycin came in 1947 when it was found to destroy some kinds of large viruses. Aureomycin was the first antivirus drug, and Dr. Paul de Kruif called it "God's gift to doctors."

Streptomycin

Dr. Selman Waksman had coined the word "antibiotic" in 1942 to mean chemicals that interfere with the life of a microorganism. Waksman worked for Merck and Company, a pharmaceutical manufacturer, and he also taught at Rutgers University. One day, one of his students brought him a new mold that he had found in the throat of a New Jersey chicken. When Waksman tested the mold, he found that it produced a substance that killed some kinds of pneumonia and infection-causing bacteria. But he was more amazed to find that it killed the tuberculosis bacillus. Everyone had hoped that penicillin would wipe out tuberculosis, but it hadn't. Here at last was a drug that could battle one of the world's major diseases. Waksman called the drug streptomycin.

Ordinarily the company that discovers a new drug has exclusive rights to produce and sell that drug, but Dr. Waksman believed that streptomycin was too important to the world to be limited to one drug company. The Merck Company agreed to give up its exclusive rights so that other companies could produce streptomycin, too.

After long use, however, streptomycin lost its power against tuberculosis. The TB bacillus had become resistant to the new antibiotic, so the search for more and better antibiotics went on.

Guinea pigs had always been used for TB testing, but in 1946 E. R. Squibb and Sons began to use a new variety of mice that were susceptible to the TB bacillus. Mice have shorter life spans than guinea pigs, and that speeded up the testing. More than 5,000 com-

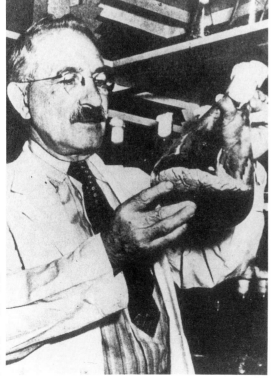

Dr. Selman Waksman coined the word antibiotic in 1942. He discovered the drug streptomycin, which was effective against tuberculosis.

pounds were made and tested on these mice at the rate of 20 compounds each week.

Five years and 50,000 mice later, at a monthly meeting of Squibb's research section in 1951, someone read a report on the effectiveness of one of the compounds. The report ended with the sentence, "None of the mice died." It galvanized the research team into action. They worked overtime and canceled vacations. When they tested and retested the new compound, they found that it was 15 times more effective than streptomycin. The Squibb Company gave it the name Nydrazid. Just as they were about to market their new product, the Swiss pharmaceutical company Hoffmann-LaRoche announced that it had a new drug called Isoniazid. The two new drugs were exactly the same.

The companies might have had a long, drawn-out, expensive legal battle to decide which one should make and sell the drug—but instead they took an almost unheard of action. They agreed to look at the chemists' lab notes. The company whose notes had the earliest date would have the patent rights, and the other company would have a license to make the drug, without paying the patent company a royalty fee. The Swiss firm got the patent by a few days, and Squibb was licensed to make and sell the drug.

Terramycin

The Pfizer company found a winner close to home. Its lab had collected soil samples from Alaska to Australia and from Africa to the Amazon. Eleven researchers studied 100,000 soil samples estimated to hold 34 million organisms per teaspoon. But one of its most important products came from a backyard in Terre Haute, Indiana in 1949. That sample held a new mold they named terramycin. At the time, penicillin was being used to fight 25 different diseases and streptomycin was effective against 15 organisms—but terramycin could combat 100 different diseases, including scarlet fever and pneumonia. Only a few months after its discovery, terramycin was in production.

Names for these antibiotics are usually taken from the "mother" organisms from which they are produced. Terramycin came from soil in Terra Haute. Miamycin is an antibiotic from soil in Miami, and Nystatin was named for the N.Y. State Board of Health laboratory where it was developed. Sometimes scientists don't stick to names of places. Doricin and Helenin were named after scientists' wives, and Seramycin was named after a mother-in-law.

Cyclosporine

The mechanics of transplanting a heart, kidney, or other organ from one human to another have been pretty well perfected. Trouble strikes, however, when the new owner's immune system senses the transplanted organ as a foreign invader and rejects it. The first drug used successfully to fight this rejection was cyclosporine. It was found in a soil sample collected in Norway by an employee who was on vacation from his job at the Sandoz Pharmaceutical Company in Switzerland. But like any drug, cyclosporine doesn't always work for every patient, so the drug makers keep searching.

A new anti-rejection drug may come from microbe FK-506, which was found in 1984 in soil samples collected by Fujisawa Pharmaceutical Company near Mount Tsukuba, Japan. The early trials of the new microbe, named *Streptomyces tsukubaensis,* have worked well for liver transplant patients.

During the years just after the discovery of penicillin, more than 5,000 different antibiotics were discovered, but only 17 of them were commercially successful. Microorganisms are constantly becoming resistant to the antibiotics used to kill them, so laboratories continue to test soil samples in search of newer, more powerful drugs.

8 BANTING'S SUMMER PROJECT

For most of human history the diagnosis of diabetes mellitus was a death sentence. There still is no cure for diabetes, yet millions of people have the disease and live normal lives because Frederick Banting had an idea he wanted to work on one summer.

Two thousand years ago, a Greek physician described diabetes as the disease that brings a "melting down of the flesh and limbs into urine . . . The patient is short-lived, for the melting is rapid, the death speedy. Moreover, life is disgusting and painful, thirst unquenchable, drinking excessive."

His description was true. The Greek name *diabetes,* meaning "to pass through," describes the symptom of frequent urination. Mellitus was added to the name by the Romans, who noticed that bees swarmed to the patient's urine, which was full of sugar. *Mellitus* is Latin for "sweet as honey."

Diabetes is not caused by a bacterium or virus. It is not really a disease, but a disorder. It is a malfunction of a gland called the pancreas. The main job of the pancreas is to produce digestive juices. But inside the pancreas are small patches of cells known as Islets of Langerhans, which secrete a hormone called insulin. Even before it had been seen, the hormone had been given the name *insulin,* from the Latin word for island. A hormone is a chemical messenger, a substance made in one place in the body and distributed by the bloodstream to stimulate some action in another part of the body.

Insulin regulates the amount of sugar in the blood. It also helps transfer sugar into cells where it will be used for energy. After you eat, the amount of sugar in your blood rises and insulin is secreted. When your blood sugar drops, insulin secretion stops, and the liver releases some of its stored sugar (glucose) into the blood. It's a delicate balancing act. When there isn't enough insulin, the glucose piles up. This excess sugar passes out of the body in the urine, which is why diabetics get little use from the food they've eaten. Diabetics get thinner, and they get thirstier because they need enormous amounts of water to dissolve this extra sugar so it can be excreted. It does seem like a "melting down of flesh and limbs into urine."

The only treatment for diabetes was a diet that was almost starvation. But if it's controlled with insulin, the imbalance can be corrected. Insulin is replacement therapy. It supplies the body with something it lacks. Many scientists had tried to find insulin. They weren't successful, because the digestive juices in the pancreas broke down the insulin before it could be separated. Dr. Frederick Banting— like others before him—knew that if he could isolate insulin in a healthy animal, he might be able to inject it into diabetics.

Frederick Grant Banting's discovery of insulin must have been one of the shortest successful research projects ever launched. And at the time, he must have seemed the most unlikely person to try it. Dr. Banting graduated from medical school at the University of Toronto in 1916, and served as a medical officer in World War I. When he returned to Canada after the war, he opened an office, but it wasn't easy for a young, unknown doctor to build a private practice. So while he waited for patients, Banting taught part-time at the University of Western Ontario medical School in London, Ontario.

He was assigned to teach physiology, the science that explains how the body works, although it was not his specialty. When he was reviewing his notes on the pancreas, he read an interesting article that gave him an idea. The article said that the pancreas would degenerate or shrivel up if the duct that delivers the digestive juices to the intestine was tied off. One night he got out of bed and made a note to himself: "Ligate the pancreatic ducts of dogs. Wait six to eight weeks for degeneration. Remove the residue and extract."

Ligate means to tie off. He wanted to tie off the duct to the pancreas and wait until the pancreas dried up. He was sure that if he removed the dried-up pancreas, there would be no digestive juices left to destroy the insulin. Then if he ground up the dried pancreas, he could feed the extract to the diabetic animals. He was certain that the extract would still contain insulin.

In the next few months, Banting read every paper he could find on such research. But he admitted later that he was far from knowing everything that had been done, and if he had known, he might have been too intimidated to try his experiments. He had no experience in this field, no money, and no laboratory—but when he discussed his idea with his friends at Western Ontario University they agreed that it might work. But they reminded him that the university had no facilities for that kind of research. They urged him to go to the University of Toronto to see Dr. John Macleod, who was head of the physiology department and who had written a textbook on diabetes.

Eagerly, Dr. Banting explained his idea to Dr. Macleod. He asked if he could have laboratory space for eight weeks and enough money to buy a few dogs. Macleod said no. Banting was disappointed, but he didn't give up. Later that year he asked again, and again Macleod turned him down. The third time Banting asked, Macleod agreed to let Banting use his laboratory, probably because he was going on vacation. Macleod also recommended two young men who might assist Banting. One was 21-year-old Charles Best, who was planning to enter medical school in the fall.

Even though Banting couldn't pay him, Charles Best didn't want to pass up the chance to work on this interesting project. Usually Best played professional baseball in the summer to earn money for college, but he had some money left from his army discharge pay, which he thought would be enough to live on for a couple of months. In May, 1921, Banting packed everything he owned into a steamer trunk and two old suitcases, loaded them into his battered old Ford, and headed for Toronto to work with Charles Best.

The small laboratory assigned to Banting was often stifling hot that summer. The dogs stayed in their kennels at night, but roamed free in the lab during the day. They were always treated like favorite pets. When Dr. Banting operated on a dog to tie off its pancreas, the dog was under anesthetic, and as it recovered, the dog was given the kind of care any human patient would receive. Banting's daily notes are full of such comments as, "Dog feeling great, frisky; runs around the room."

In the first operation, Dr. Banting tied off one dog's pancreatic duct with catgut. He waited seven weeks, expecting the dog to develop diabetes, and then he planned to give the dog the extract from its own dried-up pancreas. Those seven weeks seemed very long to Banting and Best, who kept busy reading and studying about diabetes.

By July, nothing had happened. The dog was healthy. There was no sign of diabetes. The problem was that the catgut had disintegrated, and so the dog's pancreas had not dried up. They tried again, this time using silk thread to tie off the pancreatic duct of a dog named Marjorie.

Success with Extract X

All that time expended, with nothing to show for it, was discouraging, and they were running out of money. The men ate almost nothing,

Dr. Frederick Banting
and Charles Best with
Marjorie, the dog
used in the 1921
experiment that proved
the existence of insulin.

(Eli Lilly and Company)

and often slept in the lab. Finally Banting sold his beloved old Ford in order to buy food for themselves and the dogs. On July 30, their luck changed. Marjorie showed all the signs of a diabetic. They removed her shriveled pancreas that had been tied off with silk. When they ground up the pancreas and dissolved it in a salt solution, they had their extract X. They called it iletin. When they gave Marjorie an injection of iletin, the dog was fine within a few hours. Her blood sugar was normal and there was no sugar in her urine. They had found a treatment for diabetes.

More Insulin

But how long could they keep diabetic animals alive? How large an injection was needed? How often? What would happen in an overdose? There were many questions to be answered, but they kept running out of the iletin. Where could they get a large supply? Banting had another bright idea. He had grown up on a farm, and he remembered that his father always bred their beef cattle shortly before they were sent to the slaughterhouse, because pregnant cows ate more and put on weight.

Banting did not want the pancreas glands from the adult cattle, but from the unborn calves. No digestion takes place in the intestines of a fetus during the first four months. So Banting believed that meant there would be no digestive juices to destroy the insulin; which was exactly what they found. A huge supply of pancreases that would otherwise be thrown away, could now be used to supply insulin.

Six months after they started work, Banting and Best used themselves as guinea pigs and injected each other with their iletin. When Macleod returned from vacation, he could hardly believe what these two inexperienced young men had done. Macleod insisted on changing the name of the hormone to insulin, because the word had been used by earlier researchers and it was easier to say; Banting agreed. Macleod added E. C. Noble and James Collip to the team, two biochemists who could work on purifying and standardizing the hormone.

In November of 1921, just six months after the project began, Banting and Best presented their discovery at a scientific meeting in Toronto. In December, Banting read a paper about insulin to the American Physiological Society in New Haven, Connecticut. He

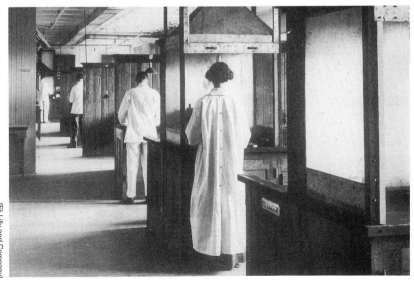

(Eli Lilly and Company)

One of the first research laboratories for insulin.

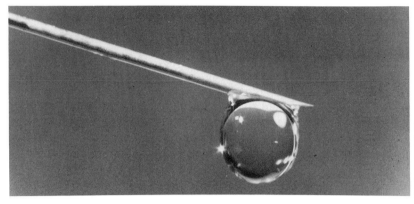

The first drop of insulin manufactured by the Eli Lilly Company.

added Dr. Macleod's name to that paper because Macleod was a member of the American organization and they were not. Dr. Macleod believed that the chairman of a department should receive the main credit for any research done in his department. When newspapers reported a speech about insulin that Macleod gave in Atlantic City, New Jersey, neither Banting nor Best were mentioned. And an article in the *British Medical Journal* gave the impression that it was Macleod who had made the discovery.

The insulin department at Eli Lilly in the early days of production.

[Eli Lilly and Company]

Ernest Eberhart was the first scientist in an Eli Lilly laboratory.

In 1923, Banting and Macleod were awarded the Nobel Prize in medicine and physiology, the first Canadians to be so honored. But Banting was furious that the committee had split the prize with Macleod, and he was even angrier that Charles Best had been ignored. Banting always went out of his way to emphasize Best's part in the discovery. After Dr. Banting gave half his $40,000 prize to Charles Best, Macleod shared his prize with the biochemist J. P. Collip.

News of insulin's magic spread fast. Doctors everywhere wanted a supply of insulin to treat their diabetic patients. The Connaught Laboratories in Canada and the Eli Lilly Company in the United States began to manufacture this wonderful drug. Dr. Banting and Dr. Best did not get rich from their discovery. Refusing to patent the drug in their names, they turned over the rights to insulin to the University of Toronto, where the funds are used for more research.

Recombinant DNA for New Drugs

In those early years of manufacture, pancreatic glands from 6,000 cattle or 24,000 hogs were needed to make a single ounce of insulin. Today insulin no longer depends upon slaughtered animals. Now it is genetically engineered and manufactured in bacteria with a technique called recombinant DNA.

DNA is deoxyribonucleic acid. It is the material that contains the genetic information in the chromosomes of all living things. DNA

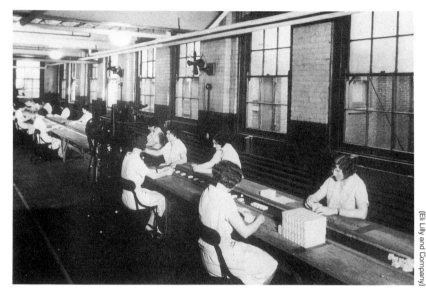

This was the packaging department for insulin in the 1920s.

holds the blueprint that "tells" each cell of an organism what it will become, what job it will do, how it will work, and what it will look like. When a piece of DNA from one organism is spliced into the DNA

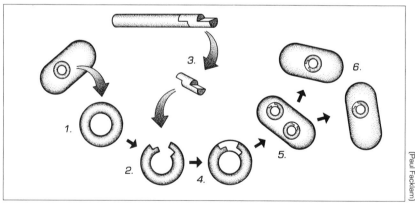

Recombinant DNA: 1. A circle of DNA, called a plasmid, is removed from a bacterium. 2. With chemicals, the plasmid is snipped open. 3. A small section of human DNA is removed from a human cell, and 4. is inserted into the open bacterium plasmid. 5. The plasmid with the human DNA section added is put back into the bacterium, where the plasmid duplicates itself. 6. The recombined bacterium reproduces with both its own and the human DNA.

[Eli Lilly and Company]

Insulin crystals produced by Eli Lilly Company using recombinant DNA technology.

of another organism, it is called recombined DNA. When the recombined DNA molecule reproduces, it passes along the genetic information in the DNA from both organisms.

An insulin-making gene is spliced into a common, one-celled bacterium called *E. coli.* The spliced bacteria grows in huge vats, multiplying by the millions, and doubling their number every 20 minutes. These bacteria make insulin as the spliced gene directs. The insulin is extracted from this bacterial soup. Producing insulin in this way is much faster and less expensive than obtaining it from slaughtered animals. The insulin produced is always the same. It never varies; quality control is built in. Insulin was one of the first drugs to be manufactured on the bacteria production line, but more and more drugs are being genetically engineered each year.

Human Growth Hormone

Not too many years ago the only way to get human growth hormone was to take it from the pituitary glands of human cadavers. It was so expensive and difficult to make that every bit of it went right to children whose bodies did not make enough of their own. There was barely enough for the 10,000 or so children in the United States who, without this extra hormone, would be dwarfs or would remain very small. But now the hormone is plentiful because the gene for making it is spliced into *E. coli* bacteria, which are grown in vats. Even more recently, a Swiss pharmaceutical company, Aries-Serono, made a human growth hormone called Saizen, which is even safer for human use because it uses a mammalian cell instead of *E. coli*. Because the cells that make it are more similar to those of humans than the bacteria cells were, Saizen is less likely to trigger the patient's immune system to reject it. The hormone-making gene was spliced into the cell of a mouse. Then production was set up with recombined mouse cells reproducing in vats of nutrient broth where they made the human growth hormone.

Growth hormones may have other uses besides helping undersized children. They seem to help severely burned children to heal faster. They help people whose kidneys fail, and they seem to reverse some of the changes that take place in the body as people age. And now there is evidence that growth hormones may even help AIDS and cancer patients maintain their weight during long chemotherapy treatments.

9 VACCINES AND VIRUSES

Vaccinations are so common that we take them for granted. In the United States, before children begin school, they are vaccinated against measles, polio, whooping cough, diphtheria, mumps, tetanus, and smallpox. Today almost no one gets smallpox, but for centuries, it was one of the most feared of all diseases. Seldom was there a family that did not lose a member to smallpox, and many who survived an attack were marked for life with faces pitted by the "pox." But it was those survivors who held the clue to the cure.

The First Vaccinations

Edward Jenner is credited with the introduction of the smallpox vaccination in 1798, but he was not the first to try it. As far back as the 11th century, healers in China and western Asia had noticed that people who survived one attack of smallpox seldom got the disease again, although they didn't know why.

In 1716, when Lady Mary Wortley Montagu was in Turkey as the wife of the English ambassador, she often watched old women going from house to house giving vaccinations. They carried nutshells filled with pus taken from people who had mild cases of smallpox. They would scratch a vein in the arm of a "customer," smear a bit of the infected fluid on the cut, cover it with a nutshell, and tie it in place. Seven or eight days later, the treated customers would come down with mild symptoms of smallpox and would recover a few days later, never to get smallpox again. Not everyone recovered, of course. The needles used to make the scratches weren't sterilized, no antiseptics were used, and people sometimes died from infections. But Lady Mary took a chance and had her three-year-old son inoculated—and it worked.

[National Library of Medicine]

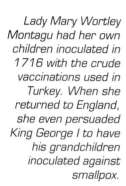

Lady Mary Wortley Montagu had her own children inoculated in 1716 with the crude vaccinations used in Turkey. When she returned to England, she even persuaded King George I to have his grandchildren inoculated against smallpox.

When Lady Mary returned to England and tried to convince doctors to use the procedure, she was told it was a "heathen" practice. Eventually she persuaded authorities to inoculate six prisoners at Newgate Prison, who were promised pardons for volunteering. When all the prisoners survived, King George I was so impressed that he had his two grandchildren inoculated. Still, these vaccinations were never completely safe. No one could predict who would become immune and who would die. A safer method was needed, and that's where Edward Jenner came in.

It was 1796 when Jenner began his experiments. Farmers knew that people who milked cows sometimes got a disease called cowpox from infected animals, but if they did, they seldom got smallpox. Cowpox caused sores on the milker's skin, which eventually healed. Edward Jenner took pus from the sores of people infected with cowpox and scratched that material into the skin of healthy people who had never had smallpox. He called it ingrafting. The people he ingrafted became immune to smallpox. Jenner had no idea what caused smallpox, nor did he have any idea of why or how the ingrafting worked.

What Jenner didn't know was that when exposed to foreign germs the body's immune system makes antibodies, which are proteins that

Although Edward Jenner was not the first person to vaccinate against smallpox and he had never seen the organism that causes the disease, he was the first to conduct experiments, and in 1798 he published the results.

fight and kill off these invaders. Antibodies are specific. Each antibody fights one certain type of germ or invader. If you get vaccinated with smallpox, your body makes smallpox antibodies that from then on fight off smallpox invaders. If you get vaccinated with diphtheria, your body makes diphtheria antibodies that protect you from diphtheria invaders for life.

A hundred years would pass after Jenner's ingrafting experiments before anyone found out about the immune system and how it works. But Jenner had brought about a near-miracle at a time when medicine was mostly a guessing game. For the first time in history, people could choose to be vaccinated and become immune to a deadly or disfiguring disease. Many chose not to, of course, because they didn't understand vaccination and because it still had risks.

Rabies Vaccine

In 1885, Louis Pasteur discovered a vaccine that prevented a disease no one could survive—rabies. Pasteur didn't know the cause of rabies, except that he knew it was caused by a germ too small to be seen with his microscope. Then Emil von Behring and Paul Ehrlich found the bacterium that caused diphtheria and made a vaccine to prevent it.

With three of the world's worst diseases—smallpox, rabies, and diphtheria—under control, people began to expect more miraculous medicines from science. But the miracle drugs were slow in coming because there was so much to learn.

Viruses

Tobacco has done little good for humans, except for the part it played in discovering viruses. In 1895, a Dutch botanist, Martinus Beijerinck, was studying a disease that stunted the growth of tobacco plants and mottled the leaves in a mosaic pattern. Trying to find how the plants got this tobacco mosaic disease, he pressed juice from infected tobacco leaves and rubbed it on uninfected leaves. The healthy plants got the tobacco mosaic disease, but Beijerinck still didn't know what caused it. He couldn't find any bacteria in this infecting juice, so he ran it through a fine porcelain filter. That should have filtered out any disease organisms, but the filtered juice still caused the disease when it was rubbed on healthy plants. Certain that there had to be an active organism in the juice, Beijerinck called it a filterable virus. He took the word *virus* from the Latin word that means poison.

In the early 1930s, Dr. Walter Reed discovered that yellow fever is caused by a filterable virus, and he made a vaccine to fight it. But still, no one had seen one of these tiny poisons that could go through a filter. Then in 1935, an American biochemist, Wendel Stanley, processed a ton of infected tobacco leaves down to one tablespoonful of white crystalline powder. When he was able to infect healthy tobacco leaves with the white powder, he knew he had isolated the unseen virus. Years later, after the powerful electron microscope was invented, the tobacco mosaic virus was revealed as rod shaped. Since then, of course, scientists have identified hundreds of viruses of many shapes and sizes.

Virus are little more than packets of genetic information with a covering of protein. But are they alive? Some scientists say yes because viruses contain DNA. Other scientists say viruses are not alive because they can be crystallized. But unlike inorganic crystals, the crystallized viruses can be reactivated. The molecules in the outer coating of the virus recognize a molecule on the surface of a living cell, and that's what determines which kind of cell it enters. Viruses are specific about where they infect an organism. Certain viruses go to the digestive system, others to the throat, or lungs, nervous system, or blood cells. Viruses are longtime fellow travelers of humans,

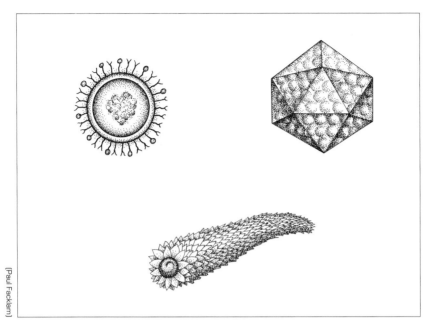

[Paul Facklam]

No one knows how many different viruses exist, but each one has its own distinct shape. Upper left is the mumps virus, upper right is the polio virus, and below is the tobacco mosaic virus.

animals, and plants. They infect every living thing, but most of them do no harm. Some last a short while, but others can lie dormant for years before they burst into action.

Some viruses become part of a person's genes and stay forever in the body. If you get chickenpox as a child, that virus may become active when you are older to give you a disease called shingles. Cold sores caused by the herpes virus may come back again and again all your life. The human immunodeficiency virus (HIV) becomes part of a person's DNA. It may lie dormant for 10 years or more before it blossoms into auto-immune-deficiency syndrome, or AIDS.

Polio

Poliomyelitis, or polio, terrified everyone in the United States and Canada between the 1920s and the 1940s. *Polio* is from the Greek word meaning gray, and *meyel* from the word for spinal cord. The disease is caused by a virus that inflames the gray matter in the spinal cord. For a while it was called infantile paralysis because it left children paralyzed and crippled. It's been around a long time. Archaeologists think that one of the Egyptian pharaohs may have had polio, because on a tomb carving he is pictured with a crippled leg.

Of 27,000 cases of polio in the first big epidemic in the United States in 1916, there were 6,000 deaths. The next epidemic struck Toronto, Canada in 1937. Hospitals were crowded with children confined to "iron lungs" that helped them breathe. No one knew how the disease spread, how to prevent it, how to cure it, or why it caused epidemics. Some doctors thought the germ was airborne and entered the body through the nose. People panicked when they heard that, and children were kept home from parks, beaches, movie houses and other crowded places. Thousands of Canadian children had their noses sprayed with a zinc sulfate solution to try to prevent the disease from entering, but it didn't work. Some children treated in this way lost their sense of smell. Later it was discovered that the polio virus multiplies in the intestines, but it either strikes the base of the brain and kills rapidly, or it strikes the lower spinal cord and causes paralysis.

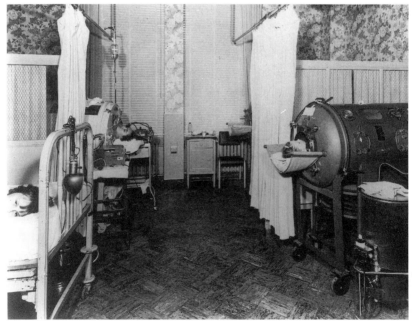

(National Library of Medicine)

During the polio epidemics of the 1940s children paralyzed by the disease were kept alive in huge metal cylinders called "iron lungs" that forced air in and out of their lungs. After the vaccine was developed, iron lungs became obsolete.

(March of Dimes Birth Defects Foundation)

Donald Anderson was the first March of Dimes poster child in 1946.

During those first epidemics, the chance of anyone making a polio vaccine was about as good as the chance of a prehistoric man inventing television. There were too many unknowns. How did the virus travel? Where did it reproduce in the human body? Polio virus had been grown in the brains of monkeys, but that limited the research. Research takes time and money—lots of money.

The National Tuberculosis Association was the first national group to make appeals for money in order to conquer a disease. People joke now about the "disease of the month" because there are so many special interest groups asking for donations. But in 1907, when the Tuberculosis Association sold its first Christmas seals, the small contributions added up quickly.

The National Foundation for Infantile Paralysis followed the TB Association plan in 1938, when Franklin Delano Roosevelt was president of the United States. The president had lost the use of both legs when he was paralyzed by polio in 1921, and he was a strong supporter of this new foundation. Using the slogan "March of Dimes" for its first campaign, the foundation asked people to send dimes to the White House on January 30, 1938, the president's birthday. Hundreds of bags of mail overflowed from the White House mailroom into hallways. Some dimes arrived taped on cards, gift-wrapped, and even baked into cookies and cakes. Across the country, porch lights were put on, and women marched house to house in the first Mothers March on Polio to ask for contributions. More than $2 million was collected that first year, and millions more year after year.

The first big breakthrough came in 1949. John Enders had been working on a vaccine for the mumps virus. He had some leftover culture medium, which had been used to grow the mumps virus, and rather than throw it away, he decided to see if he could grow some polio virus he had kept frozen. No one had ever tried growing it in this medium, made of bits of chicken embryos and ox blood. Enders was surprised when the polio virus grew and reproduced. It was one of those small steps that give research a big boost.

There are two different kinds of vaccine. One kind is made from a "dead" or inactive virus and the other from a "live" or active virus

[March of Dimes Birth Defects Foundation]

President Franklin D. Roosevelt and March of Dimes president Basil O'Connor count dimes that were sent to the White House in 1938 to raise money for research on poliomyelitis.

that has been considerably weakened. Some scientists believed that a dead virus lost all or most of its immune power and would not stimulate the body to make antibodies. Others were afraid that a live virus, no matter how weakened, might cause polio.

Salk's Vaccine

Jonas Salk, a scientist who had helped found the March of Dimes, believed in a killed-virus vaccine. He isolated three strains of polio virus, killed them with formaldehyde, and injected them into monkeys. When he tested the monkeys later he found no live polio viruses, but the monkeys had built up lots of antibodies. It was the result he had hoped for, but it was no guarantee of the same reaction in humans.

By 1952, Salk's vaccine was ready to test on humans. Like most scientists then, he gave it to himself first. Then he injected his wife and three sons with the new vaccine. Next he gave the vaccine to 45 children who had polio because he knew they would already have built up antibodies, and they would be safe if by any chance the vaccine was harmful. Tests on all these people showed no sign of the live polio virus, but lots of antibodies against it.

Between 1940 and 1950, when polio struck in a series of epidemics, a great public outcry to use a vaccine had developed and the sooner the better. By the time Salk's vaccine was ready in 1952 there was a lot of public pressure. Two large pharmaceutical companies, Eli Lilly and Parke Davis, were chosen to make the Salk vaccine for the first trials. Never before had an experimental drug been given to so many healthy children. People worried. What if all the virus weren't dead? Would thousands of children get polio from the vaccine? Could vaccinated children pass the polio on to unvaccinated children? Would the vaccine really make children immune? Faced with these terrible possibilities, strict regulations were set on the trials. Each batch of vaccine made by the two companies had to pass three tests, one at the manufacturer's lab, one at Jonas Salk's lab, and one at the laboratory at the National Institutes of Health.

On April 26, 1954, first-, second-, and third-graders from selected schools across the nation lined up to get the first of three shots of Salk vaccine. Thousands of volunteer nurses, doctors, and parents helped with this huge project. Employees of the medical equipment union stopped their strike to go back to work to make enough hypodermic needles and syringes. It was a double-blind test, which means that no one knew until after the test results were in who got the vaccine and

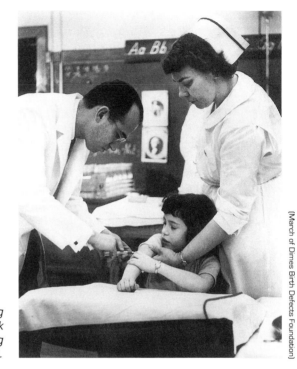

Dr. Jonas Salk giving an injection of his Salk polio vaccine during field trials in 1954.

(March of Dimes Birth Defects Foundation)

who got a placebo. Only the foundation had the code. A placebo is a fake. In this case, it was a harmless solution tinted the same color as the vaccine. Polio vaccine was given to 441,000 children, and 201,000 received a placebo. More than 1 million other schoolchildren were part of the experiment as the "observable control." They received neither vaccine nor placebo but were carefully watched for any symptoms.

The results of the test were announced a year later on April 12, the anniversary of President Roosevelt's death. The vaccine was 70 percent effective against type I polio virus, and 90 percent effective against both types II and III virus. It was 94 percent effective in preventing paralysis of the lungs and death. The public went wild when the news was announced. Church bells rang across the nation, sirens screamed, and signs appeared everywhere saying "Thank you, Dr. Salk." Two hours after the announcement, the vaccine was licensed and available to everyone.

All the pharmaceutical companies geared up for production of the vaccine in the summer of 1955. Five million children were vaccinated, but 250 of those children got polio and 11 of them died. The vaccine given to 150 of these children had come from a batch made by the Cutter Pharmaceutical Company. As soon as it knew, the company withdrew its vaccine. Somehow live polio virus had showed up in the vaccine, undetected in the safety checks. The other 100 cases seemed to be children who just did not build up an immunity or who had already contracted the polio virus before their vaccination. Despite these tragic cases, the vaccine was considered a success.

Sabin's Vaccine

While Jonas Salk had been developing his dead virus vaccine, Albert Sabin had been working on a live polio virus vaccine. Sabin had graduated from medical school in 1931, the year that polio crippled or killed 6,500 children in New York City. In 1935, he grew a strain of polio virus in a culture of human cells. The three vaccines against major diseases—smallpox, rabies, and yellow fever—were made from live viruses, and Sabin was certain that a live, but weakened, virus would give long-term immunity for polio, too. And it would be cheaper and easier to give because it wouldn't have to be injected. It could be eaten.

By 1957, Sabin had a vaccine made from the three kinds of live polio viruses. But where would he test it? Most American children had already been vaccinated with the Salk vaccine. Sabin knew there had been several outbreaks of polio in Russia, and he got permission to test it there. During the next two years, Sabin gave live vaccine in sweet syrup or candy to children in Russia, Poland, Mexico, and Singapore. Fifteen million children were vaccinated, with very few ill effects. In 1960, the surgeon general of the U.S. Public Health Service approved the oral Sabin vaccine, and within three years, more than 70 million American children had eaten sugar cubes containing Sabin vaccine.

The whooping cough vaccine that has been used for decades is made from dead pertussis bacteria. Most children in the United States are vaccinated before they are three years old, usually at the same time they are vaccinated for typhoid and diphtheria. Even so, whooping cough affects about 4,000 American children each year. Worldwide, it strikes 60 million children and causes about a million deaths. Some experts believe that the vaccine itself can cause brain damage, although there is no proof of that yet. An Italian scientist has genetically engineered the pertussis bacteria to remove the toxic portions that cause the bad side effects. His new vaccine hasn't been tested on

(March of Dimes Birth Defects Foundation)

Dr. Albert Sabin administers his easy-to-take Sabin oral polio vaccine to the Bennett family in 1959.

children yet, but it may turn out to be safer than the vaccine now in use.

In 1980, when United Nations health officials found that only 20 percent of the world's children had been vaccinated against the big killer diseases, they started a major campaign. Ten years later, 80 percent of all children in the world under age one had been immunized, and millions of lives had been saved.

Vaccines are the best of all drugs because they stop a disease before it starts. Jenner's smallpox vaccine must have seemed miraculous because suddenly, and for the first time in history, people were safe forever from a disease that could wipe out whole towns. But the future of vaccines may be even more amazing.

Dr. Steven Rosenberg, at the National Cancer Institute, said in an interview in 1991, "When you think of a vaccine, it's usually to prevent a disease." But he believes he may have found a way to vaccinate cancer patients against their own cancer as a way to cure it. He goes on to explain, "Here we're actually treating an advanced cancer." The procedure is still an experiment. But even if it doesn't live up to Dr. Rosenberg's hopes, the research is a giant step toward finding a vaccine that can keep cancer at bay.

10 STARTING FROM SCRATCH

We need cures for cancer, AIDS, Alzheimer's, arthritis, schizophrenia, depression, the common cold, and dozens of other diseases and deficiencies. Where does a pharmaceutical company start when it decides to make a new drug?

Millions of chemicals can be combined and mixed in a million ways, but without a clue or a lead to follow, drug makers would have better luck looking for a needle in a haystack. One pharmaceutical company says that out of 2,000 compounds studied, maybe 200 will show some possibilities in early tests. Of that group maybe 20 will reach the stage of testing on people, and only one might be found safe and effective. Others say the number might be more like one in 10,000. All this research and testing takes time; it may be 10 years before the new drug is even sent to the Food and Drug Administration (FDA) for approval. And it will cost between $200 and $300 million to take the drug from the first idea to the finished licensed product.

There is no standard way to come up with a new drug. Each drug has its own story. "What is required, though," says an executive of one pharmaceutical company, "is good science building on good science."

When Paul Ehrlich was looking for a cure for syphilis, he knew from previous research that arsenic kills the syphilis spirochete. That was his lead. But he tested 606 different arsenic compounds in hundreds of combinations before he found the one that worked.

An American Chemical Society publication says that pharmaceutical research today consists of "mimicking natural products, . . . screening likely chemicals, chance observations, astute questioning, and unexpected turns."

Most drugs have come from chemicals that mimic natural products. Chemists can isolate the active ingredient in plants, fungi, animal cells, and human cells to make a drug. Then they can pattern a similar drug—or a better one—from other chemicals. All drugs, from the greenest brew of a witch doctor to the most potent substance concocted in a laboratory, are chemicals. There is no difference between a "chemical" medicine and a "natural" one. People who buy vitamin C tablets made from rose hips are getting the same vitamin C that is made from the raw chemicals.

Screening for Drugs

Before World War II, American doctors used quinine to control malaria, but during the war, pharmaceutical companies couldn't get the bark of the chinchona trees to make quinine. The federal government sponsored research to look for a substitute. Chemists synthesized and screened more than 60,000 substances until a lab found the one that worked, chloroquinine phosphate. The synthesized drug was more potent and less toxic than quinine, and it could control malaria with a once-a-week dose. But a new report from the Institute of Medicine says that drug-resistant strains of malaria are increasing, and new research is needed to look for yet another drug to control this disease, which strikes more than 100 million people each year.

Screening for a drug discovery is a long, tedious process. The researchers don't know what they'll find, but there's always a chance of stumbling on something worthwhile. Who knows what might be sitting on a shelf waiting to be discovered? Cyclosporine sat on a shelf for two years before an immunologist ran it through more screenings and found that it could help a transplant patient's immune system fight the rejection of a new organ. AZT was the first drug approved by the FDA for AIDS patients, but it wasn't intended for that use. It had been designed to treat cancer, but it wasn't very effective as a cancer drug. It, too, was shelved until someone decided it might be useful against the AIDS virus and put it through more tests.

Even if a chemical is only slightly effective against a disease organism, or is effective but a bit toxic, that chemical can be altered. One atom taken off or added on to a molecule can change the way that chemical works. Most drugs that came from natural sources may have been altered in this way.

Animal Testing

One way of screening is to test chemicals randomly in mice. During 35 years of injecting more than 400,000 different chemicals into mice with leukemia at the National Cancer Institute, 36 drugs were approved and licensed.

Not all human diseases infect animals, and not all drugs work in all animals. Penicillin was poison to guinea pigs. Rats weren't affected by thalidomide. Mice don't get polio, AIDS, or Alzheimer's disease. Without an experimental animal, research can be severely set back. Early in the science of medicine, bacteria were grown in petri dishes, and the test chemicals were applied directly to the bacteria. That was the case in testing penicillin and the other antibiotics. But viruses can grow only in living cells, and it was not until the 1940s that someone found a way to grow live human cells that could be inoculated with viruses. Now it's standard procedure to test chemicals on viruses and bacteria growing in these human cell cultures.

In the late 1980s Dr. Solomon Snyder, a professor at John Hopkins School of Medicine, discovered a way to grow human brain cells in vitro for the first time. In vitro means the organism is raised on nutrient material in a flask or other container. In vivo means the organism is grown in a living animal. The in vitro growth of brain cells was a giant step for research because these cells, called neurons, do not divide and grow like other cells, and testing always had to be done in live animals. Brain research will move ahead much more quickly now.

There's a lot of controversy about using live animals to test drugs, but there's little choice. Would it be better to test new drugs directly on humans? Not likely—who would volunteer for that? Scientists worry about the stress and discomfort to experimental animals as much—or more—than animal rights people do because they are the ones who have to do the tests and take care of the animals. But these scientists know that without animals, there would be few of the cures and wonder drugs we take for granted. Every reputable drug company uses as few animals as possible and works hard to make sure they are treated humanely and properly cared for.

One of the first organizations to give research money to scientists who could find ways to run experiments with fewer animals was the Johns Hopkins Center for Alternatives to Animal Testing. The center funds one scientist who is trying to develop a line of human kidney cells that can be grown in vitro. She is studying the effects of environmental and chemical poisons on kidneys, and she hopes to do it without having to sacrifice countless small mammals in the first stages of the research.

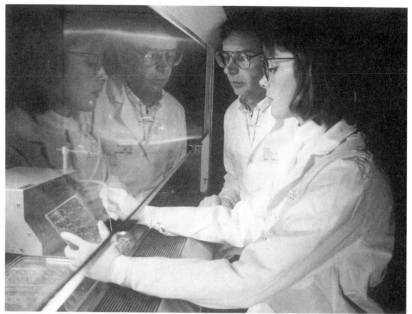

These scientists at the Eli Lilly company are involved in a cancer research project to refine a technique for growing certain solid tumors in the laboratory and then test different compounds on those tumors.

When the National Cancer Institute began to use automated devices and computers to test possible cancer-fighting drugs on real human cancer cells, rather than on mice, they found they could test more than 300 chemicals a week. And they've reduced their use of animals by 95 percent. Over the last seven years, Hoffmann-LaRoche Inc. has decreased its use of animals in drug tests by 67 percent.

But testing chemicals in culture dishes and test tubes is not the same as testing them in a whole living organism. Remember Prontosil? That drug killed streptococcus bacteria in the human body, but it did not kill the same bacteria in a test tube. Prontosil was broken down by enzymes in the body, and only then was its active ingredient, sulfanilamide, released. Usually it's the other way around. New drugs far too often work only in the test tube stage, and fail in humans.

Eventually, a drug must be tested in animals. In an animal, a chemical may not even get to the disease organism. It may be absorbed by other tissues and excreted. If its taken by mouth, the chemical may not be absorbed into the blood stream from the digestive system, or it may be broken down by natural enzymes.

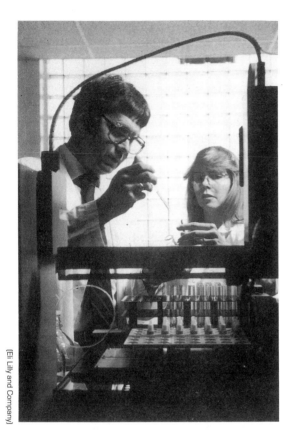

Today's pharmaceutical companies employ teams of scientists who discover and develop new products.

Transgenic Mice

A drug might work in the culture dish *and* in the experimental animal but not in a human. The biology of humans and other mammals is similar, but it's not exactly the same. There are drugs that will cure all types of cancer in mice, but those drugs don't work on humans in the same way.

But what if human genes could be grafted into mice? Wouldn't that be a way of finding out in early tests how human cells react to new drugs? It would, and since the development of the "transgenic mouse," it is. These animals are not science fiction. A transgenic animal is one that carries new genes called transgenes. Genes can be taken from any species and inserted by microinjection into the fertilized egg cell of another species. The new genetic material, DNA from a human, for example, can become part of a mouse's DNA, and will be inherited by the offspring produced by that mouse. The method is similar to recombining DNA from an insulin-making cell into *E. coli* bacteria.

Transgenic mice can now be used to study diseases that could only be seen in larger animals before. For example, mice do not get a disease called hepatitis B, but chimpanzees do. Now, hepatitis B transgenic mice can take the place of chimpanzees in studies of that disease. Other transgenic mice have been produced that are supersensitive to carcinogens, or cancer-causing substances. It's easier to detect the presence of carcinogens in the environment with these supersensitive transgenic mice, which means that researchers won't need to use as many animals as they once did to find the cancer hazards.

Alzheimer's disease (AD) research has been slow and expensive because the disease could be studied only in older primates. That meant keeping chimpanzees and monkeys in labs for years. There was no such disorder in rodents until an AD transgenic mouse was developed. Now Alzheimer's can be studied in whole generations of mice in a matter of months instead of years. No one knows just how much these transgenic animals will mean to biomedical research. But they are certain to bring major changes in the study of aging, birth defects, cancer, allergies, autoimmune diseases, infectious diseases, and environmental health.

Computer-Designed Drugs

Many drugs these days are designed by computer. Once a scientist knows the molecular structure of the targeted virus or bacterium, a computer can help find a magic bullet drug to combat it. A hundred years ago, Paul Ehrlich knew that a drug must fit into a receptor on the cell just as a key fits a specific lock. It was a simple idea, and he had no way of knowing just how specific that fit would be.

Biologists have made use of incredible equipment from chemistry, atomic energy, and basic physics research to help them find the structure of molecules. They use radioisotopes to track molecules through any living organism. They use chromatography to separate and identify chemicals in complex mixtures, and infrared and ultraviolet spectroscopy to identify compounds in living tissue. Nuclear magnetic resonance (NMR) produces images through a computer that show changes as they are happening in living organs. Tiny electrodes, smaller than a hair, can monitor the movement of material in and out of a single cell. And X-ray crystallography can reveal the exact structure of a molecule.

An engineer uses equipment called liquid chromatography columns to purify human insulin.

All living things are chemical factories. Thousands of chemical reactions are taking place in each of our cells continually. If even one essential reaction stops, the cell can die. But each chemical reaction needs a catalyst, something to get it going. These are the enzymes, and there are thousands of them. They are specific proteins that help a reaction without being used up in the reaction. Each has a different molecular shape, and the shape determines the enzyme's activity. Food in the stomach and intestines has to be broken down into the simplest compounds the body can use. That's the job of digestive enzymes. They catalyze, or start, the reactions that break down food. Without them, a pizza would remain pizza in your stomach, and even the most nutritious food would not get to your cells.

Each enzyme is specific for one reaction. One part of the enzyme molecule fits a specific structure on the molecule of the reacting chemical. If it doesn't fit, nothing happens. If scientists don't know the molecular structure of the disease organisms and of the chemical drug, not much happens either. The more they know about each molecule, the better chance they have of designing a drug to fit it.

Engineers can design buildings because they know the amount of stress different kinds and shapes of metals and wood will stand, or the amount of weight a certain kind of arch will support. So it is with

Dr. Thomas Swann designs the molecular shape of new drugs at his computer at Westwood-Squibb Pharmaceuticals, Inc. in Buffalo, New York.

(K. C. Kratt, photographer)

medical chemists. They know the architecture of molecules. They can build them to work as they want them to work, most of the time. It's a long, tedious, complicated process. One drug designer said, "Don't make it sound too simple or too easy because it's not."

After the structure of an enzyme molecule from the disease organism has been seen with X-ray crystallography, the data is put into a computer and the image of that molecule appears on the screen. Then the drug designer can turn it around and view it from all angles. The idea is to design another molecule that will fit the disease organism enzyme and inactivate it, like putting a sheath on a knife or a guard on a chain saw. That new molecule will be an effective drug.

But that's only part of it. If the new drug will be taken orally, it must be designed so it won't be digested. It has to pass directly into the bloodstream. The new drug must not be broken down or changed by other enzymes as it moves through the body, or excreted before it gets to infected cells. This drug is going to go into every cell of the body, even the ones that are not infected with the disease. If you take an antibiotic to get rid of an infection in your finger, the drug doesn't go just to that finger. The bloodstream takes it on a complete circuit so it reaches every cell. If that drug molecule binds with any human enzymes, instead of just the disease enzyme, there can be side effects. A side effect might be nausea, or dizziness, or a rash, or a headache, or a dozen other symptoms.

Paul Ehrlich was firing blind when he found salvarsan because he couldn't see the target molecule. Today's scientists can not only see the target but they can pick out its most vulnerable spot and design a bullet that hits the bull's-eye. A drug designed in this way has a good chance of being both effective and safe.

11 WHO SAYS IT'S SAFE?

In the United States, a drug isn't safe until the Food and Drug Administration says it's safe.

A drug called thalidomide changed the drug business in America. When thalidomide was sold for the first time in Germany in 1953, it was greeted as the best nonprescription sleeping pill the world had ever seen. It induced safe, deep, natural sleep, with no danger from overdose because it contained no barbiturates. It was even added to aspirin and cough syrups for children. Women were overjoyed because thalidomide solved the age-old problem of morning sickness in the first months of pregnancy.

In January 1959, the American pharmaceutical company William S. Merrell obtained a license to make thalidomide under the brand name of Kevadon. Following legal procedures, they filed a New Drug Application (NDA) with the Food and Drug Administration. By April 1961, Kevadon was available through doctors in Canada, and it looked as though it was going to be an important drug in America as well.

Dr. Frances Kelsey was the investigator at the FDA assigned to review the Kevadon application. She was in no hurry to make a decision, especially when she began to hear frightening reports drifting in from Europe about babies born without arms or with flipperlike limbs and deformed bodies after their mothers had taken thalidomide. In November 1961, Germany took thalidomide off the market, and a few days later, so did Great Britain. The Merrell company notified Canadian doctors to stop prescribing Kevadon to pregnant women or to any woman old enough to have a baby. But Merrell still urged Dr. Kelsey to review their application with an open mind. Fortunately, she did just that. She studied the data again and again, but she refused to give her okay. Finally, in April 1962, the Merrell company withdrew the Kevadon NDA.

Between 1959 and 1962, more than 3,000 thalidomide-deformed babies had been born in Germany alone. How could a company be so wrong in making a drug? For one thing, thalidomide wasn't wrong. It was very effective for all people, young and old, male and female. It was even effective for pregnant woman—effective, but not safe. The *testing* had been wrong! The tests had been done on rats, and rats do not produce deformed babies even on high doses of thalidomide. But rabbits do. If rabbits had been used first, perhaps the drug would have carried a warning and the tragedy would not have been as great. It was the rats that were the clue to Dr. Kelsey that something wasn't quite right. She kept going back over the studies, wondering why the rats didn't get sleepy on thalidomide when it was a sleeping pill. Clearly it did not affect them.

On August 7, 1962, President John F. Kennedy awarded Dr. Kelsey the Distinguished Federal Civilian Service Award for "her high ability and steadfast confidence in her professional decision."

After the FDA hearings on thalidomide, Senator Hubert Humphrey, who had been a pharmacist before entering politics, said, "The United States this time escaped by the skin of its teeth, so to speak." Senator Estes Kefauver proposed a bill, which Congress passed into law,

President John F. Kennedy awards the nation's highest civilian honor to Dr. Frances Kelsey for her work in keeping the dangerous drug thalidomide from being sold in America.

[Food and Drug Administration]

ordering pharmaceutical companies to prove that drugs are both effective and safe.

FDA Standards

An effective drug is one that does the job it was designed to do—kill specific bacteria or change a body function such as blood pressure. A safe drug is one that has as few side effects as possible. No drug is perfect because each person who takes it may react differently to the drug's ingredients. A drug can be effective but kill a patient. A drug can be safe to take but may not cure the disease or check the problem. When drugs pass the FDA requirements, they have passed both requirements.

The Food and Drug Administration does not test drugs. That must be done by the manufacturer. After a pharmaceutical company has made a new drug, it has to find out if it works before it can ask the FDA to review it. The first step is called preclinical testing, and that takes at least a year or two. These studies by the drug maker answer the questions: Is the drug biologically active? Is it safe? Does the drug

[Food and Drug Administration]

FDA investigator Ann deMarco watches a three-story spray dryer in a formulation room. She also checks blenders and other equipment to make sure drugs are being mixed at the right speed and temperature. She must know if 30 minutes is the proper time for blending a certain medication, and not 20 or 40.

do what you hope it does? These first tests are never done on humans, but always on animals, beginning with mice, rats, or hamsters, then on dogs, and finally on primates.

Researchers must find out how fast the drug gets into the bloodstream, how fast it is distributed to the rest of the body, how fast it is used by the cells, and how fast it leaves the body.

If Dr. Banting were looking for insulin today, his May-to-December testing would never pass FDA standards. He didn't begin with mice or rats, but used dogs right from the start because he was getting the insulin from the dogs. Nor did he test insulin on primates. He went directly to a human trial, using himself as the guinea pig. Earlier scientists too had tested their discoveries on themselves first. They seemed to believe that if they had no faith in their own medicine, how could they ask someone else to try it? Paul Ehrlich tried the syphilis-fighting salvarsan first. Florey and Chain injected themselves with penicillin. Jonas Salk gave himself an injection of his polio vaccine and then gave it to his three sons. Dr. Sabin took his oral polio vaccine and gave it to his children, too. But that wouldn't happen now. The rules of drug development are made to protect everyone, including the drug makers.

Once the animal studies are completed, the sponsor files an Investigational New Drug application (IND) with the FDA. A sponsor can be an individual, a partnership, a corporation, or an agency of the government such as the National Cancer Institute. A drug is new if it fits into one of these categories:

1. It is composed of a new substance, either an active ingredient or an inactive one, such as a coating.
2. It is a new combination of already approved drugs.
3. It is a new formulation or ratio of active ingredients already on the market.
4. It is an approved drug offered for a new use.
5. It is an approved drug with a proposed new dose or new method of taking (liquid instead of pills, for example) or duration of use.

The application for an IND must show the chemical structure of the drug if it is known, its action in the body, its effects, and its safety. It must also describe the details of manufacturing it. The FDA has 30 days in which to *disprove* the information. If the drug maker doesn't hear from the FDA, it moves on to the three phases of clinical trial in humans.

Human Trials

Phase I: 10 to 20 healthy adult male paid volunteers are recruited for these first human trials. These men are usually between the ages of 18 and 45. Older people aren't used because they may be on other medications, or they may have known or unknown medical problems. Women are not usually included in this first human test because they might be pregnant or might become pregnant during the test, and no one wants to put an unborn baby at risk. Products made specifically for women, of course, are tested on women. Often companies advertise for volunteers at colleges, among hospital personnel, or at prisons. One company that needed volunteers for a month put an ad in a writer's magazine, offering young men a small salary, room and board, and a quiet place to write in exchange for trying the new drug.

All the volunteers must sign consent forms. Tests are never done on people without their permission. That wasn't always true. In the past, drugs were sometimes tested on prisoners without their knowledge. In the 1930s, more than 400 men in a public health study were examined and diagnosed as having syphilis. It's doubtful that many of them even knew they had the infection or understood how they might be treated. They received no treatment. Instead, they were "studied" over the next 40 years, just to follow the course of the disease, even though many were suffering considerable pain.

Elderly patients in a New York hospital in 1963 had cancer cells injected under their skin as part of a study of immunity. No one told them what the injections were, just that their resistance was being measured. Fortunately, the test was stopped soon after it began, and none of the patients got cancer. Patients rights are now protected by law. The FDA has a videotape for volunteers that explains that they can stop or leave the study at any time for any reason. "Informed consent" means more than just signing a paper. The researchers must explain what the study is about, and answer all the volunteers' questions to make sure they understand what to expect.

These first human tests will show whether or not the drug is safe, and how a person tolerates different doses. After a volunteer takes the drug, he or she is tested at regular intervals to see how fast it is absorbed into the bloodstream, how fast it is distributed, metabolized, and excreted—in other words, how long it takes the drug to move through the body. Many drugs are dropped after these tests because they aren't well tolerated, or aren't safe, or simply don't do anything.

If the drug passes Phase I, it is moved to Phase II, which will tell if the drug does what it was designed to do. Before they begin the second phase, some clinical study teams from the manufacturer meet with FDA reviewers to ask questions and discuss potential problems, although it's not required. In Phase II, the drug will be given to 20 to 100 patients who have the disease or condition the drug was made to treat. Researchers will look for side effects, and for how well patients tolerate the new drug. When this data has been collected and reviewed, the drug maker will be ready to move to the largest test, Phase III.

The FDA requires two well-controlled studies for Phase III, using as many as 3,000 patients who have the disease the drug is meant to treat and who are in the care of fully qualified doctors in hospitals or clinics. These studies will test the strength and effectiveness of the drug at different doses. They are called double-blind or placebo studies. A placebo does nothing. It may be a pill or capsule that looks like the real drug but contains nothing more than sugar or starch. A double-blind study is one in which neither the person getting the drug nor the person giving it knows which is the real drug and which is the placebo. None of the nurses or doctors knows which patients are getting the real drug and which are getting the fake one. Placebos are *never* used when patients are being treated with antibiotics or cancer drugs. Those patients are either given the new drug or they continue on the treatment they've been using all along. Once the studies are over and the drug has passed all the tests, volunteers who took the placebos are sometimes offered the new drug free for as long as they need it.

Phase III may last for three years or more. "The length of clinical trials depends largely on the kind of drug being studied," says one FDA report. It goes on to say, "A drug to treat relatively common infections that is meant to be used only for a few days or weeks may get through all three clinical trial phases in two to four years. On the other hand, a drug for high blood pressure that patients may take for decades could be in the clinical trial phase for seven to eight years or more to thoroughly assess its long-term effects."

When the third phase of testing is over, the company is ready to prepare and submit a New Drug Application (NDA). This is the big one—literally big. All the information collected in the studies must be sent to the FDA. It's not unusual for a company to ship a truckload of thousands and thousands of pages of data to Washington, D.C. In this ton of paperwork the FDA reviewers must find information from all phases of testing. They look for the chemical structure of the new drug, its purpose, all the animal and laboratory studies, the results of all human studies, the details of the drug formula and how it will be manufactured, packaged, and labeled.

Then the company waits. Two or three years may pass before the FDA investigators send their answer. During this time, FDA may ask questions that the manufacturer's clinical team must answer. The FDA has been harshly criticized for the long delays, especially in the review of desperately needed drugs. Patients drying from cancer or AIDS or some rare disease are willing to try anything, even the most experimental drugs that haven't been thoroughly tested. They have nothing to lose. So the rules have changed. Now doctors can get experimental drugs for a patient with a life-threatening disease, or for a patient who is allergic or resistant to the usual treatments. These unapproved drugs are called "compassionate" or "treatment" INDs (Investigational New Drugs).

Under pressure from many groups, the FDA speeded up the investigations on AIDS drugs such as AZT (azidothymidine). On March 20, 1987, FDA approved AZT as safe and effective for helping certain patients with AIDS and advanced AIDS-related disorders. It was the

[Food and Drug Administration]

Each year, FDA investigators inspect about 5,000 of the 18,000 drug manufacturers to see that medicines are being made under proper conditions. Here investigator Ann deMarco checks bulk containers of raw materials.

shortest review on record, less than four months. More than 4,000 patients used AZT during the investigation. But the FDA emphasizes that " . . . no drug is absolutely safe. There is always some risk of an adverse reaction. It's when the benefits outweigh the risks that FDA considers a drug safe enough to approve."

AZT is not a cure for AIDS. It has serious side effects. Former FDA commissioner Dr. Frank Young said, "We want the public to know and understand that miracles don't happen overnight, that studies take years, not months, and that patients are best served by rigorous testing and careful review."

In October 1991, a second AIDS drug, called ddI, was approved for patients not helped by AZT. For two years, more than 22,000 Americans with AIDS were given ddI at no cost even before the clinical trials on the drug were finished.

Even after the New Drug Application is approved and the drug is on the market, the drug company must send reports to the FDA four times a year to evaluate the drug's long-term effects. They must give further details about the production of the drug, how its quality is

An FDA inspector confers with an official from the plant being inspected. The Food, Drug, and Cosmetic Act authorizes the inspection of factories, warehouses, establishments or vehicles "and all pertinent equipment, finished and unfinished material, containers and labeling."

(Food and Drug Administration)

controlled, and where the drug has been distributed. It's the same careful pattern set by Paul Ehrlich almost a hundred years ago.

There are two other "watchdogs" that keep track of the drug business. Each hospital, clinic, or other institution where the testing takes place has a review board that monitors the clinical trials as they progress. And the FDA sends inspectors to check the pharmaceutical company's labs and factories.

A manufacturer can hold a patent on a new drug for 17 years. When that time is up, other drug companies can make the drug with minor changes and under a different name. It's an advantage to consumers if a dozen drug companies make a dozen different kinds of aspirin, for example, because individuals react so differently to medications. One person might get an upset stomach from one brand of aspirin, but find another brand easier to digest because it is coated with some soothing ingredient. One person might tolerate a liquid medicine that another person would rather take in a capsule. And with more than one similar drug on the market, the prices are more competitive, too.

A company advertises and promotes a new drug aggressively because it has only a few years in which to earn back the $200 to $300 million it spent to make that drug before there is competition. A manufacturer usually applies for the patent during the first year or two of a drug's development in order to protect its rights, even if there's no certainty that the drug will work out. If it takes the average 12 years to create and test the drug, the company has only five years left on the patent—five years in which to earn back its enormous investment before other companies can make that drug. A company can ask for an extension of the 17-year patent, but it's not easy. A senator must stand up in Congress and request it.

No-Name Drugs

Some companies make no-name or generic drugs. These are products that have the same ingredients, the same safety as the original brand-name drug, and undergo the same manufacturing process. But the FDA rules allow a leeway of 20 percent above or below the original drug's effectiveness. The store-brand or no-name aspirin, for example, has the same ingredients and it's made the same way as any of the brand-name aspirins, but it's cheaper because you're not paying for packaging, advertising, or added ingredients such as buffers or coatings. Druggists can fill prescriptions with generic drugs, if they are available, to replace the brand-name ones.

Today, potent drugs are handled under sterile conditions. In these "clean rooms" workers must wear special masks and clothing.

Orphan Drugs

An "orphan drug" is one made to treat a rare disease. About 2,000 diseases fall into this category, which is defined as a disease that affects fewer than 200,000 Americans. Like any other manufacturer,

In 1991, bottles of medicines are filled on an assembly line under truly sterile conditions.

a drug company is in business to make money. But making a drug to treat a handful of people won't begin to earn back the millions of dollars spent in creating that product. In January 1983, Congress passed the Orphan Drug Act, which gives pharmaceutical makers some help. They can claim a tax credit and apply for grants to pay for some of the research if they make an orphan drug. They are guaranteed seven years' exclusive use of the orphan drug, during which no one else may sell it in the United States.

Pharmaceutical companies are not like manufacturers of chairs or pens or shoes. They must meet the requirements of good medicine and good science, as well as good manufacturing.

12 BACK TO THE FUTURE

Tropical rain forests are disappearing faster every day. What does that have to do with drugs? Everything—scientists are certain that hidden in the forests are hundreds of possible medicines and foods. But as these forests are mowed down, the plants and animals that live there are becoming extinct faster than we can find out about them. Edward O. Wilson, a biologist at Harvard University, estimates that the loss of plant and animal species doubled between 1979 and 1989. He believes we may be losing anywhere from 4,000 to 40,000 species each year.

The drug manufacturer Merck, Sharp & Dohme has signed a contract to give $1 million to Costa Rica in exchange for the rights to develop drugs from plants and animals found in Costa Rican forests. The million-dollar down payment will be used to train people to collect samples of shrubs, trees, fungus, microorganisms, insects, lizards, frogs, and anything else that might possibly yield some active ingredient for a new drug.

Cancer Drug in the Forest

In a vast program to screen natural compounds, the National Cancer Institute found a cancer-fighting drug called taxol in America's northwest forests. Taxol is made from the bark of the Pacific yew tree. It shrinks tumors, especially in ovarian cancer, and kills cells in a way that researchers had never seen before. Taxol stops cells from forming a kind of scaffold, which they need when their halves pull apart as they divide. It's been called one of the most important new cancer drugs in 15 years. Unfortunately, the drug makers are up against environmentalists, and it's a tough choice—which is more important, saving endangered forests or saving lives?

The bark from three yew trees can supply enough taxol for only one patient. Before it can be harvested, a tree has to be at least four inches in diameter, which means it is 70 to 100 years old. In 1991, the National Cancer Institute asked for enough taxol to run tests on 12,500 patients. That meant cutting down 38,000 trees to get 750,000 pounds of yew bark. Lumber companies consider the yew trees useless for timber anyway, and they often burn off whole tracts of them to get to the more valuable trees. On the other hand, using these slow-growing trees for taxol could lead to their extinction very quickly. That's the bad news. The good news is that further research may have found two ways to have it all—both trees and taxol.

At the University of Florida, Dr. Robert Holton found a substance called baccatin III in the needles of the ornamental English yew shrub. He combined baccatin III with a synthetic chemical to get taxol. Using this sturdy common shrub would eliminate the need to kill a tree by stripping its bark. Instead, the needles are stripped, but they grow back. Dr. Holton says that with his process only two pounds of needles produce enough baccatin to make taxol for one patient.

Another possibility, of course, was to synthesize taxol—make it from chemicals in a laboratory. But after 10 years of trying, chemists found that taxol's complex chemical structure was just too hard to duplicate. So researchers turned to a technique called tissue culture to grow Pacific yew bark cells. With this method, it may be possible to create a "forest" of taxol-producing bark in a laboratory without cutting down a single tree.

In the first step of tissue culture, small pieces of bark are cut out and put in trays of nutrient-rich gel, where the cells grow into a mass called a callus. Cells from the original callus are used to produce more cultures and more callus. After several weeks, the callus is harvested and dried, and the taxol is extracted.

Ancient Medicine Made New

The future of drug making seems to lead backward in time. More and more pharmacologists are turning to the medicines used by ancient healers. They are looking past the myths and superstitions to track down the active ingredients in the old remedies. One example is chaga, which is a Russian folk medicine used to treat stomach cancer. Chaga is made from tumors found on birch trees. Chemists at The Upjohn Company in Kalamazoo, Michigan are trying to isolate the birch tumor's active ingredient.

Dr. Robert Schultes, a botanist at the Botanic Museum of Harvard University, spent years in the Amazon basin, searching out the plants used for medicines by native people. He believes that probably fewer than half the compounds produced by plants have been identified and tested as possible drugs. That's true of animals as well.

Ground-up seashells, sponges, and coral starfish from Australia's Great Barrier Reef are being analyzed for chemicals that might fight cancer. One scientist has called the 18-inch giant Amazon leech a "veritable living pharmacy"—researchers have only begun to find everything it might produce. The same is true of snake venoms, toads' skins, and fish.

If you've ever picked up a fish, you know how slippery it is. Most fish secrete a coat of slime beneath their outer skin. But the slime secreted by the Arabian saltwater catfish is no ordinary slime. It's a gel-like substance secreted on the fish's outer surface, and it can heal wounds. Biologists think that the catfish probably developed the slime as a way to heal itself quickly because a bleeding fish attracts predators. The slime coats the wound and protects it from dirty water.

Dr. Richard Criddle, a biochemist at the University of California at Davis, was studying marine life in the Arabian Gulf when he cut his hand. He smeared the cuts with catfish slime, and they healed in three days instead of the usual eight to 10 days. When the slime was analyzed, it was found to contain 60 different proteins that help heal wounds. Some drug companies are interested in working with catfish slime to see if they can develop a medicine that might speed up the healing of sores and wounds of diabetics, burn victims, AIDS victims, elderly patients, and other people who don't heal well.

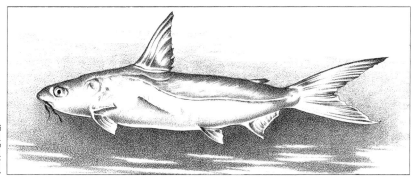

(Paul Facklam)

The gel-like slime that coats the Arabian saltwater catfish contains 60 different proteins that may yield new drugs that will help heal burns and wounds.

Dr. Tom Eisner, an entomologist at Cornell University, believes that all insects should be screened for useful drugs. He says that this kind of "chemical prospecting" has already turned up insects that produce cortisone, steroids, and some anti- viral compounds.

Two American pharmaceutical companies are trying to bring back a notorious drug from the past. Thalidomide, the sedative that was pulled off every market in the world 30 years ago, is once again up for review by the FDA. Once scientist calls it both an angel and a devil of a drug. Its devilish part is well known, but new research shows that thalidomide can help patients accept bone-marrow transplants. It also helps people who have rheumatoid arthritis and lupus. Thalidomide is available through the U.S. Public Health Service, but only for treatment of leprosy or Hansen's disease. If the FDA okays it, new clinical trials of this old drug will begin again. Of course, if it is approved, it would never be prescribed for pregnant women.

Return of Diseases

Smallpox was wiped out by vaccinations—or so it seemed. Measles had disappeared—or so it seemed. Forty years ago we thought that antibiotics had stopped tuberculosis—but now there's a worldwide epidemic that has caused 3 million deaths. In 1990, 23,000 Americans were diagnosed with tuberculosis. Many age-old diseases, once cured or at least held at bay, are coming back. One public health worker said that getting close to wiping out a disease, but not quite getting it all, may be worse than the disease. When people think a disease is conquered, there is a tendency to cut back on preventive measures. Why spend money preventing something that doesn't seem to be a threat? Over the years, new drug-resistant strains of bacteria and viruses appear, and there is a general decrease in natural immunity because fewer people have been exposed to the old diseases and developed defenses against them. That means that researchers must look for new vaccines, new antibiotics, new antiviral drugs to combat the old diseases.

Transgenic animals will play a big part in our future. Cows will deliver drugs with their milk. Just as *E. coli* bacteria mass-produce insulin and growth hormones, other drugs can be spliced into the milk-making genes of cattle, and extracted later from the milk. Several biotechnology companies have plans to genetically engineer sheep, goats, pigs, and cows to manufacture two important human blood-clotting agents.

Crops of transgenic plants may be even more valuable than animals, especially for drugs that are needed in huge quantities. Scientists have used a microbe called Agrobacterium to transfer human DNA into plants. They even have a "gene gun" that shoots the DNA into leaves. Now a field of sugar beets or potatoes can turn out enormous quantities of serum albumin, which is a human protein that's needed during surgery.

One biotechnical company has made a sunscreen by combining human melanin with plant cells. Melanin is the substance that gives color to our skin. It is better than ordinary sunscreens at scattering the ultraviolet rays of sunlight that cause sunburn.

The anticancer drug vincristine, made from the periwinkle plant, is expensive. It costs thousands of dollars to produce and isolate just one pound of vincristine from plants raised on plantations in Madagascar. One fire or hurricane or plant disease could wipe out the entire crop. But if the gene for vincristine were inserted into tobacco plants, it could be grown and harvested more cheaply on hundreds of farms in this country.

There may be endless possibilities for new drugs and new ways of making them. One might imagine all sorts of "miracle" drugs, but most drug makers would settle for such miracles as a cure for cancer, AIDS, Alzheimer's disease, or the common cold. Only research will solve those problems; there's no other way. In the meantime, pharmaceutical companies will continue to make the thousands of useful drugs we have learned to depend upon and trust—painkillers, tranquilizers, anesthetics, cough and cold medicines, blood pressure medicines, vitamins, vaccines, hormones, anticonvulsants, antidepressants, antibiotics, and many others.

GLOSSARY

Antibiotic a compound made by a living organism that kills bacteria or stops their growth.

Antibody a protein produced by white blood cells that recognize and destroy or deactivate a specific foreign molecule.

Atom the smallest part of an element that has the properties of that element. It is the building block of all matter.

Bacteria a one-celled form of life that is smaller and simpler than plant or animal cells and does not have an organized nucleus.

Cell the basic unit of structure and function of living things; the smallest unit that can carry on the activities of life.

Chemotherapy the treatment of a disease by the use of chemicals that have a specific and direct effect on the disease.

Chromatography a process that can separate and identify individual substances in a complex mixture.

Control group the organisms (such as the cells, animals, or people) in an experiment that are not exposed to the factor being tested.

DNA deoxyribonucleic acid, the molecule in cells that contains genetic information in the form of a code.

Elixir a sweetened liquid containing alcohol mixed with some medicinal substance.

Emetic a substance that causes vomiting.

FDA the Food and Drug Administration, a department of the United States federal government that oversees the safety and effectiveness of drugs as well as food.

Generic drug a "no-name" drug that is not protected by a trademark registration but is a copy of a drug that does have a trademark.

Hormones special proteins produced by glands and carried by the blood to regulate specific reactions in other cells; for instance, insulin, which is produced by the pancreas to regulate the level of glucose in the blood.

Infrared spectroscopy a process that measures the wavelengths of invisible infrared light that are absorbed or reflected by an object.

It is used to study the molecular structure of complex organic compounds.

In vitro a phrase that means in an artificial environment, such as a flask or test tube; a substance may be tested or cells grown *in vitro.*

In vivo a phrase that means in a live organism; a substance may be tested or cells grown *in vivo.*

Molecule a chemical unit made up of two or more atoms held together by a chemical bond.

NMR nuclear magnetic resonance, a process that develops images from the biochemical operations of the body by measuring their nuclear magnetic field.

Nostrum a medicine recommended by its maker, but without any scientific proof of its value or effectiveness; patent medicines are nostrums.

Orphan drug a drug made for a small number of people who have a rare disease.

Pharmaceutical a medicinal drug. A pharmaceutical company manufactures medicines.

Pharmacologist a person who searches for new drugs and studies the safety, effectiveness, and manufacture of drugs.

Pharmacopeia an official list of standard drugs, and how they are prepared and used.

Placebo an ineffective and harmless substance used in controlled experiments for testing the safety and effectiveness of another substance.

Poultice a soft, moist mass of substances applied to the body for medicinal purposes, such as treating an infection.

Protozoa one-celled animal-like organisms that have a nucleus.

Purge to rid the body of unwanted substances by vomiting or bleeding.

Radioisotope a form of an element that gives off high-energy radiation.

Recombinant DNA a combination of part of a DNA molecule from one organism with the whole DNA molecule from another organism.

Synthesize to make a substance that does not occur naturally; to make in a laboratory.

Transgenic refers to the transfer of genes from one organism to another.

Ultraviolet spectroscopy a process that measures the wavelengths of invisible ultraviolet light that are absorbed or reflected by an

object. It is used to measure the concentration of a substance in
solution.

Vaccine a substance that will cause an immune response to a disease;
the vaccine can be dead or live weakened disease organism that
causes the person's immune system to make antibodies.

Virus an extremely small, simple infectious agent that can grow and
duplicate itself only in a living cell. Typically a virus is composed
of DNA or RNA (ribonucleic acid, like DNA, is a molecule that
can make up a gene) surrounded by a protein coat.

X-ray crystallography a process that uses X rays to determine the
chemical structure of compounds that are in a crystalline form.

FURTHER READING

Burger, Alfred. *Drugs and People*. Charlottesville, Va.: University of Virginia Press, 1986. An overview of pharmacology written in everyday terms with a minimum of technical jargon.

Dobell, Inge N., ed. *Magic and Medicine of Plants*. Pleasantville, N.Y.: Reader's Digest Association, Inc., 1986. Good illustrations add to the interesting stories of medicinal plants.

Edelson, Edward. *The Immune System*. New York: Chelsea House Publishers, 1989. A basic book on the human immune system written for young adults.

Evon, Carol. *The Virus that Ate Cannibals*. New York: Macmillan Publishing Co., 1981. Six medical detective stories about the search for the viruses that cause polio, colds, cancer, and other diseases.

Griggs, Barbara. *Green Pharmacy*. New York: The Viking Press, 1982. Full of interesting stories about the history of medicines.

Hancock, Graham, and Carim Enver. *AIDS: The Deadly Epidemic*. London: Victor Gollancz Ltd., 1986. The story of worldwide research on AIDS.

Harris, Seale, M.D. *Banting's Miracle: The Story of the Discovery of Insulin*. Philadelphia: J. B. Lippincott Co., 1946. It's an old book, written by a man who knew Dr. Banting, and well worth looking for. Many libraries still have it.

Hobby, Gladys L. *Penicillin: Meeting the Challenge*. New Haven, Conn.: Yale University Press, 1985. This has a lot of technical information, but you can skip those parts and enjoy the story of penicillin development in America written by one of the people who did the research.

Jacobs, Francine. *Breakthrough: The Story of Penicillin*. New York: Dodd, Mead and Co., 1985. A fascinating account of the development of penicillin, written for young people.

Kerrins, Joseph, M.D., and George W. Jacobs. *The AIDS File*. Woods Hole, Mass.: Cromlech Books, Inc., 1989. A review of the research being done on the AIDS virus and the search for drugs to stop it.

Marks, Geoffrey, and William Beatty. *The Medical Garden.* New York: Charles Scribner's Sons, 1971. Another fascinating book about healing herbs and other plants that have been used as medicines.

Marquardt, Martha. *Paul Erlich.* New York: Henry Schuman, Inc., 1951. This is an old book, but fascinating because it was written by Dr. Erlich's secretary. Some libraries still have it.

Sneader, Walter. *Drug Discovery: The Evolution of Modern Medicines.* Chichester, N.Y.: John Wiley and Sons, 1985. This is quite technical and a reader would have to be well versed in chemistry.

Steiner, Richard P., ed. *Folk Medicine: The Art and Science.* Washington, D.C.: American Chemical Society, 1986. An easily read book full of interesting anecdotes about medicines made from plants and animals.

White, Peter T. "The Poppy," *National Geographic* 167, no. 2 (February 1985): 143–189. An in-depth look at the history of the plant from which opium, morphine, codeine, and heroin are derived.

INDEX

Italic numbers indicate illustrations

INDEX

T

Talbor, Robert 8
taxol 103–104
tea 1
terramycin 56
thalidomide 83, 91–92, 106
Thomas, Dr. Lewis 18
tobacco 107
tobacco mosaic virus 72, *73*
toothaches 11
Toronto (Canada) 74
Toronto, University of 60–61
transgenic 85–86, 106, 110
Treasury, U.S. Department of the 26
truth serum *See* scopolamine
trypanosome 31, 32
tsetse fly 31
tuberculosis 1, 5, 22, 30–31, 55, 106
Turkey 69
Tylenol 12
typhus 53–54

U

ultraviolet spectroscopy 110–111
United Nations 80
Upjohn, Dr. W. E. 25
Upjohn Company 25, *27*, *28*, 104

V

vaccinations 69–72, 80
vaccines 9, 69–80, 106, 111
vinblastine 8–9

vinca rose *See* periwinkle
vincristine 8–9, 107
viruses 54, 72–73, *73*, 111 *See also specific viruses*

W

Waksman, Dr. Selman 54–55, *55*
Walpole, Horace 2
Washington, George 17
whooping cough 79
wild ginger 3
William Swain's Panacea 20
willow bark 1, 2, 5
Wilson, Edward O. 103
witchcraft 1, 3
Withering, Dr. William 6
Wood, Alexander 13
World War I 7, *7*
Wright, Sir Almroth 43

X

X-ray crystallography 86, 88, 111

Y

yellow fever 20, 72
yew 103–104
Young, Dr. Frank 98

Z

Zalles, Gregorio 54
Zuni Indians 3